How to Detect
FAKE ANTIQUES

How to Detect
FAKE ANTIQUES

JOHN FITZMAURICE MILLS

ARLINGTON BOOKS *London*

HOW TO DETECT
FAKE ANTIQUES
first published 1972 by
ARLINGTON BOOKS
(Publishers) Limited
38 Bury Street, St. James's
London, SW1
Printed by
The Garden City Press Limited
London and Letchworth
© *John FitzMaurice Mills 1972*

ISBN 85140 139 2

CONTENTS

Acknowledgments .

THE AUTHOR WISHES TO THANK ALL THOSE WHO
have assisted in the preparation of this book, and is indebted to
the following for permission to publish the photographs: Mr.
Kiddell of Sotheby's; the Trustees of the British Museum; Robson
Lowe Ltd.; the Research Laboratory for Archaeology, Oxford,
and the article in *Archaeometry* (S. J. Fleming and E. H. Sampson,
Archaeometry, **14,** Part 2, 237–44), the Public Record Office and
the Controller of H. M. Stationery Office; the Doerner Institute,
Munich; John Shearlock, Esq.; the National Museum of
Antiquities for Scotland and Nuclear Enterprises Ltd.; the
Victoria and Albert Museum; and the Institut Royal du
Patrimoine Artistique, Brussels.

1 *The Fascination*

NO ONE KNOWS AND IT IS UNLIKELY THAT THEY WILL EVER know what percentage of fine art and antiques is totally genuine. To a degree the whole situation is blurred by a discreet veil of secrecy. Now and again there is a bright flash of publicity as a master forger is uncovered and then the curtain drops once more.

The staccato rap of the saleroom hammer totting up the ever increasing figures must beckon to the practitioners in the dark, who by chance, circumstance or design are not out there in name. The tempting finger drags them in to supply that seemingly insatiable demand. Total records from the studios of the great, production lists of known factories are far from complete. Periods exist in the lives of artists and craftsmen which appear barren. Disasters have occurred but how much did they truly destroy. From earliest times copies have been commissioned and still are. The jungle is dense. It is almost inevitable that the first group of good fakes from a particular operator are going to bring a reward for their maker.

In early Roman times there was a wave of status collecting, a repetition during the Renaissance and now today it has all flared up again. Salerooms fight for the spoils. Antique shops proliferate down nearly every street. In part this is a signal of revulsion against the mediocre, the multi-versions of the computer controlled machines that spill out today's products. A piece of genuine age and quality brings with it an enticing sensation. This has many roots. The eye can enjoy aesthetically the colours, the lines, the form. The touch can sense the finish on an exquisite piece of carving. But most of all ownership can bring a feeling of closeness with the craftsman or artist who first created the unique or limited piece, and an association with previous owners plus the potent atmosphere of history.

How much is the forger the dark-child of affluence? Looking back he does seem to flourish with the rest of the jackals that stare enviously towards the rich man's fire.

It is not that he has been able to go unpunished. In England the statutes dealing with the subject have been legion. In 1562 the crime of forging a signature was punishable in lower degrees by a fine and at the other end of the scale by being pilloried, having both ears cut off, the nostrils slit-up and seared, forfeiture of land and perpetual imprisonment. From 1634 the executioner held the final penalty as was found out by the Reverend Dr. W. Dodd when he forged Lord Chesterfield's name on a bond. Today the severity of the punishment seems to have suffered a decline. Han Van Meegeren who totted up a total of over £700,000 for his Vermeers and others, received a sentence of just one year.

What is a forgery? In law the crime only comes out in the open when the maker of the fake disposes or sells his production. The actual private making of a forgery is not illegal. An illegal fake starts when an attempt is made deliberately to imitate another's work either by copying a known example or by creating an object in the manner of and then passing it off as original. The forger may take a known period or produce a work which supposedly fills in a gap in an artist's evolution, as was done by Van Meegeren with his spurious Vermeers. The latter course can be the most difficult to uncover. The situation can get further out of hand when genuinely commissioned copies start their journey down through history. They pass from collection to collection, come on to the market, linger on gallery walls, and somewhere along the line their provenance becomes embroidered. Romantic figures who have owned them add prestige. False certificates may have been given them and signatures added.

The best invitation card for the forger comes from the

collector who gets caught up in a vogue, who sees not the work of art or craft but only the lure of a great name. Beside him is another who lays himself ignorantly on the block, he is the one who will naively follow an assumed natural flair and go for the temptingly offered bargain. A shield for the forger is that those who do eventually find themselves lumbered are all too often loath to admit their mistake. It is an affront to their vanity and so the faked painting, vase, chair, or what-have-you lingers on in their collection. After several generations the wretched story repeats itself and the deceitful object can deck itself again in spurious glamour.

What is it that turns an often accomplished performer into a forger? In many cases it will be the good earthy reason that the person has been overcome with greed as he reads the high figures obtainable for works of art that he consciously knows he can imitate. It can be the bending of a mind or the getting back at authoritarian knowledge. It can many times be the satisfying of an ego, a personal battle with talent unrecognized. It can be an act of innocent joy, a pleasure in creating as with Dossena. His undoubted technical abilities were exploited without his knowledge by a ruthless dealer.

Strangely enough the proverbial man in the street is not startled when a new art forger is uncovered, not that is in the way he would be by a story of someone making imitations of banknotes. If anything his reaction is liable to be one of amusement. He reads that learned dignitaries have been fooled, that institutions have bought worthless bronzes or pots. The forger to him is not really in the criminal class. He is surrounded with a sense of mystery of almost wizardry. Probably the only question asked is why when these objects are uncovered is there such a disparity between their value and that of the real thing.

Further to the above should be included two other categories of the forger, the political and the psychological. An example of the former is the well-known treason case that was centred on the unfortunate Captain Dreyfus. He was arrested and charged in 1894 on the evidence of a letter, which he was supposed to have written to the German Military Attaché. The contents of this stated that the author of the letter was supplying reports about the French Army. The captain was dispatched, mainly on the evidence of a hand-writing expert, to serve a life-sentence. It was after persistent struggles that Madame Dreyfus with the help of another expert was able to force an issue. Major Esterhazy and Colonel Henry eventually confessed to the crime and Captain Dreyfus received his pardon.

Farther back in history was the involved case of Mary Queen of Scots. In January 1567 the queen had taken a convalescent Lord Darnley to a house in Kirk o' Field close to Edinburgh. On 9 February she left him to attend a party at Holyrood Palace. A few hours later at two o'clock in the morning of 10 February the house in Kirk o' Field was blown up and the body of Darnley was discovered in a neighbouring garden, strangled. Later in the year Mary was to marry the Earl of Bothwell. In July of the same year, estranged from all her friends, she abdicated in favour of Prince James. In May 1568 she crossed into England and gave herself into the protection of Queen Elizabeth I. Later Elizabeth ordered an inquiry into the death of Darnley. One piece of damning evidence was a silver casket of letters that was produced by the Earl of Moray. These he stated had been found under Bothwell's bed. The contents of these underlined that Mary had been a part of the plot to murder Darnley. None of the letters was addressed, dated or signed. Mary firmly denied the authorship of the letters. By many it is thought that they were forgeries set as a trap for her. Further the letters were never produced for Mary to see.

The literary forgeries of Thomas Chatterton (1752–70) shed a light on the workings of a deranged mind. The poet in his early years lost himself in a half world of the long past medieval. Knights' tombs with their inscriptions and oaken chests in the muniments room of St. Mary Redcliffe in Bristol became his playthings. An old illuminated musical folio taught him his letters and a black-letter bible his reading. Contacts looked on the child as mentally sub-normal. From his earliest years it appears that he was subject to outbursts of weeping and periods of near trance. Consciously or not he was slowly immersing himself into a period and more than this into the minds of the earlier scribes. A powerful imagination drove him on. A prodigy of letters he was contributing to *Felix Farley's Bristol Journal* at the age of eleven. But the romantic dream of the past was carrying him away. Before he was twelve he wrote the first of his mystery pieces from the earlier centuries. This was 'Elinoure and Juga', which he showed to Thomas Phillips, who was usher at Colston's Hospital, where he was at school. From a study of John Kersey's *Dictionarium Anglo-Britannicum* he picked up a style that was to be used in the production of works by one Thomas Rowley a priest in the time of Henry IV. It was almost as though he became the familiar of Rowley. In all some half dozen manuscripts by Thomas Rowley appeared in a slightly disguised version of Chatterton's own hand-writing. Apparently the most he received for his 'reconstructions' were a few pence. He tried to get them published but failed and as an act of desperation sent the manuscripts to Horace Walpole claiming that the contents had been found in a chest in St. Mary Redcliffe. Walpole for a time was convinced of their origin, but later was to recant. Chatterton in spite of all drew himself out of his time and literally became Rowley. So much so that when he found only rejection from his contemporaries he swallowed a lethal dose of arsenic and water. After his suicide Walpole was to denounce him as 'a lad who, they do not deny, forged poems in the style of Ossian and 50 other things'.

Is there a single motive that can thread all the fakers together? In a clear cut sense there is not. Yet deep in the recesses of their minds there is a tenuous cord. Some part of their nature warped by an incipient sense of defeat provides a strong power-drive to create. A temporary hallucination may take the forger so that he can travel up and down the paths of time and enter the mind and hands of some artist or craftsman. It may not be as deep as this, yet with many of the 'top' forgers who have come to light there are pointers to this line of thought. Yet the master forger must perforce do without the sweetness of true success in creating a great masterpiece. He must, if he is to continue, linger in the shadows; perhaps imbibing some slightly sour pleasure as his piece does deceive and have plaudits showered upon it. But it must take a hard swallow not to be able to stand beside it and share in the acclaim. At times the temptation is too great and there arises an act of self-denunciation which does not really have a parallel in any other branch of crime.

For every true forger, that is one who starts from scratch and creates his object with all the technique and skill of the original master, there must be a fair-sized pack of the lesser hands. These take old damaged pictures and turn them into some saleable work of a 'master'; they bodge together furniture fragments, and literally at times murder what could be quite a good piece. They will often rush in to satisfy a vogue for a particular period or category of objects being sought by the collectors.

How is a fake first betrayed? It is unlikely that science with all its aids is going to be the original informer, unless the culprit is tripped over during some research not necessarily directed at this purpose. The processes and techniques of science have no seeing eye. In practically every case of a forgery uncovered it has been the aesthetically trained and aware human eye which has started the chase. Stylistically is where the forger goes wrong. All the art history in the world cannot implant the individualistic bravura of a great performer. Whereas a master in the line of Frans Hals can slash in a potent free stroke, the forger not having this assurance must feel his way. Part of the answer with any great work is that it has come into being at the height of the master's powers, when he the creating artist has got beyond the strictures of technique and works with a full-blooded freedom that pulses with life and achievement.

A forgery is akin to a 'chancer'. Look the 'chancer' straight in the eye and he seldom convinces for very long. The mind begins to nag at whatever story he is trying to put over. Doubt comes in and will generally drive on until the 'fake' person is unmasked. So it is when an eye aesthetically trained comes to rest on a forgery. It may be at first there is no more than a vague feeling of uneasiness. This can be purely a mental doubt not a visual one at all. But gradually the mist will clear and the rapier of experience and knowledge will go through the deception. It is at this point that the cold ruthless dissection by scientific analysis can be called in to substantiate the opinion formed.

One favourite ploy for the forger or his agent is to surround the object with a mass of provenance. Dates, famous owners, articles that have been written about it, sale prices of long ago can be confusing and can also sometimes take quite a bit of sorting out. Labels from genuine articles can be transferred to the spurious. The paper build-up can have as much care lavished on it as the object itself, it may even at times have been going on for years.

A well restored item presents a feeling of care and possible worth. Someone must have valued it to have gone to the expense. Here is an excellent smoke-screen for the forger. He can use all his skills to produce that exquisite piece of 'Meissen', to fabricate a 'Chippendale' chair, to paint an early 'Flemish Master' on a wooden panel. Then bracing himself can deliberately smash the lovingly made pieces. Now he becomes a restorer and puts them altogether again, not forgetting to leave just a few signs of his second craftsmanship. For the unwary, he can have given the object a badge of respectability. It may double his overheads but the take should be large enough to make it worth the trouble.

The forger like any other crook all too often makes that one mistake that catches him. There can be anachronisms with dress, utensils, architecture and design. In pictures pigments are used that had not been invented when the supposed artist was working. Casting processes are used that are out of date for the period. It is one of those strange quirks of human endeavour that a man will go to inordinate pains with every other facet of the work and then leave himself wide open by some naive oversight.

Yet assuredly on will go this merry battle of wits between the collector, the expert, the scientist and the forger. Events in the past have proved that the field is wide for deception. There is the seemingly infantile mummified mermaid made from a monkey and a fish's tail. The horn of a unicorn which was nothing more than the horn of a narwhal. In Guillaume Rondelet's *Libri de Piscibus* 1554–5 there was a woodcut of the Sea Bishop, which was known as the Jenny Haver. William Blake probably used this unlikely monster as a model for his Leviathan which was an illustration for the VIIIth of Young's *Night Thoughts*. Sea Bishops are still being made today from skates. Practically every field that is burrowed through by the collector has been worked over by the gentleman bent on deceit and gain.

When it comes to the disposal the forger and his coterie are prepared to go to almost any length. It may be as simple as slipping the objects into a small sale or series of sales, as was done in 1971 with a number of reasonably expert productions of English and Continental Schools, which all emanated from a studio in Spain. At the other end of the scale can be the dreaming up of a complete atmosphere, in reality faking the arrival of the piece. It has been known that successful approaches have been made to titled figures who will allow the fraud to be placed in their castles or what not and follow this up with verbal assurances that the chair has stood there for years, or that the particular painting has never left the family since it was acquired by an ancestor from the original artist. This ploy is assisted by the general aroma of 'cloak and dagger' that hangs around 'art' discoveries. Experts, hunters for the salerooms, and the rest move about under a fair cover of secrecy.

For the hapless tyro collector the choice is set around with many snags. Apart from the 'genuine' products of the forger, as has been mentioned, there are countless innocent copies dating well back into history. These can be met with today sailing under fine titles of originality. If these are contemporary with the artist, and the student or commissioned copyist has used the same canvas, paints or materials as the master, they can cause at the least confusion. There have been and still are pastiches produced. Here artists often of considerable standing 'lift' features from several works by others and combine them. This can occur with not only pictures but also pieces of sculpture and other objects.

Today there is a growing trade in reproductions. Not just paintings, or furniture but it seems anything in the antique field, from warming pans, to Staffordshire china, from door-knockers to military equipment. All right as they come pristine and gleaming from their place of origin. But what will be their

. .

position in fifty years time when the wear of years has softened their newness, and polishing has brought up an exquisite patina, and the odd dent and scratch has aged their surface?

If expert opinion is not always on tap what is the best protection? Undoubtedly study of the chosen field is the key. Through books and visual appreciation in museums and galleries slowly can be built up a personal feeling for the genuine. This can be composed of not only a love for the beautiful and rare, an understanding of the materials and techniques but also in the final phase an intimate relationship with the master or craftsman. Couple this with humility and you will be as aware as you can be.

2 *The Artist*

IT WILL BE A LONG TIME BEFORE THE ARGUMENTS AND wonder subside that followed the exposure of Han Van Meegeren, a comparatively unknown who shook the art pundits and experts of his time. His fortune-producing success rested first and foremost on an implanted desire for vindication. But to this was coupled a study of technique, a knowledge of art history, and a skill at simulating the work of another.

The forger may be highly skilled or downright impertinent in his attempt. Elementary cases point at times to a disdain for the victim's ignorance. The con-man, for that is what a forger is, relies on several characteristics in his customer. He hopes that his avarice for the product will over-ride judgement based on study and advice. Across the whole field of collecting there rises the temptation of lucrative gain for the bent skilled hand. Anything the collector seeks is the magnet for some character to have a go. It may be old masters, today's masters, print-makers even down to the humble matchbox label. Sadly at times the sure knowledge that an item is a fake can even work in reverse. At a recent sale of stamps in Basle 257 lots of known forgeries went under the hammer to bring in over £8,000. These were the work of the late Jean de Sperati, one of the world's most accomplished producers of bogus stamps. He in his time must have had some sense of refinement, as he always mentioned his miniature masterpieces as 'imitations'.

A specialist of this rank would never have had the cheek to produce such blatant examples as the gentleman who has been issuing maps under the pretence that they are by the English cartographer John Speed born in 1552 at Farndon in Cheshire. Speed published one of the most popular series of English county maps in the early part of the seventeenth century. A specimen by his twentieth-century familiar purported to be of Herefordshire. It was printed on seemingly the right paper. The publishing date was engraved as 1622. The illusion was however quickly shattered by holding the print up to the light when the name of a well-known paper-maker of this century and the date 1964 could be read. Admittedly he had done his best to age the paper by perhaps the use of weak cold tea and a smoky candle and a little judicious weathering.

A primary safeguard when collecting is to have as deep a knowledge as possible of the ways and methods of the masters and craftsmen being sought and to profit by the exposures of forgers already known. This alone cannot be an iron-clad protection but it can do much to give warning sounds. A study of art history coupled with a knowledge of techniques can often raise that rankling doubt that something is not quite right.

Oil paintings seem to have a universal prestige over other media. Yet in some ways by their very construction they are the most vulnerable for imitation. An oil is a sandwich of several materials. The base on which it is painted is termed the support. This may be either a wooden panel or some form of canvas. If it is of wood, this can be made from a number of timbers, either in panels up to two inches thick or at times a bare quarter of an inch. Adze marks on the back are no sinecure; it is quite simple to use the tool today. Nor are worm holes a sign of the age of the painting. An old worm-eaten piece of wood can quite simply be procured by the forger. In fact worm holes exposed lengthwise along their run can be a warning. There has been the classic case of a picture on a wooden panel made up of several pieces of timber, all worm-eaten. It could be clearly seen how these holes stopped abruptly at a cross member and then reappeared the other side. Oversight, carelessness or over confidence by the trickster?

Before the artist starts to paint on his panel he must first apply a ground. With many of the early examples this ground would be of gesso. This material consists of a plaster mixed with a glue which was often rabbit's skin. The gesso would generally be applied in several coats, sometimes up to a thickness of an eighth of an inch or more. A preliminary foundation for the gesso was sometimes provided by a piece of linen or canvas glued first on to the wooden panel. The gesso sets very hard and was normally abraded down to a silk smooth surface. On this the artist could work with his individual method of paint application. This might be 'alla prima', the painting of a picture in a direct manner in one sitting, or the gradual building up with several paint layers.

An oil on canvas is carried out by first sizing the support and when this is dry applying a ground or priming that is generally a coat of white lead paint. Today this priming can be emulsion. There have been examples of gesso priming although these are rare and not good practice as they are liable to crack with movements of the canvas. After the paint has dried thoroughly the picture is varnished. Up to about 1960 the varnish used was generally one prepared from a natural resin such as Copal, Damar or Mastic. All of these tend to darken and to crack with time, features that are helpful to the forger, as they would cover up much that was beneath. In fact artificial cracking of varnish can be induced by brushing over the surface of a tacky layer with a water-soluble hoof glue. Once the varnish has hardened the glue can then be removed. Paint layers will crack quite naturally with time, changes of temperature and humidity. The forger can assist this process by careful heating and by tight rolling of the canvas. He may also attempt to paint in a crack pattern although, this last will generally be exposed by the use of a strong magnifying glass.

A device that is common with faked oil paintings on canvas is to reline them before issue. One of the difficulties for the forger is to obtain period canvas, particularly if he is aping a master from several centuries back. To get round this, after he has completed the fraudulent picture he can stick it, canvas and all, on to another support. This will be done probably with a strong resistant adhesive that will be difficult to remove, which will not only hide the original canvas he has used but also suggest to the unwary that the painting has been restored and thus must be authentic and of value. With the same thought in mind the practitioner may also deliberately damage his finished work and then restore it.

One of the hardest nuts for the forger with painting is to be able to simulate the brush strokes of the artist he is at work on. Here again the use of a glass will tell much. The study of authenticated master works will soon show how individual is the 'hand-writing' of each artist with his brushes. This can be affected by the type of brush, soft hair or bristle, the way it is held and by the consistency of the paint being used. Compare the fluid strokes of Rubens or Augustus John with the staccato stabbing of Van Gogh; the 'sweetened' surface of some nineteenth-century painters with the highly emotional manner of Soutine or Vlaminck or heavily loaded impasto of De Stael.

With the authentic work there will always be a sense of freedom and originality that the forger must aim at. Whereas the master works away concentrating on his conception, composition, colour, light and shade; the forger must do all this and added to it must all the time be conscious that he must ape the stroke type at every touch of his brush. It is this feature that has been the up-ending of many lesser lights in the game as their products tend to have a forced stilted manner against that of the artist they are trying to copy.

The faker of pictures seems to have tried almost every artifice in the manner of technique, false provenance and discovery. There could still perhaps be room for the ultimate twisted genius; and he would have to be just that, to go the whole way and manufacture a hitherto unknown master, complete with works, life story, provenance, patrons and all. This would be quite an operation if it were to be threaded into the history of art without being discovered, but someone will probably have a try when all other methods dry up. One who tried this was Peter Thompson. But first let us look at Van Meegeren who released upon an unsuspecting public his 'Vermeers' which he carefully painted in a manner that could have been in an assumed period of Vermeer's production that the experts were expecting to turn up one day.

As a specimen case of the picture forger Van Meegeren provides a comprehensive example for study. His background, his mental make-up, fastidious technique, the art scene of the thirties and his final exposure offer a complete lesson in deception.

Han (Henricus Antonius) Van Meegeren was born on 10 October 1889 at Deventer in Holland. His early years were spent in a household that was dominated by the presence of his father, a strict puritanical schoolmaster who forbade the young boy to even speak in his presence unless spoken to. When he began to draw, his father tore up many of the examples and ordered his mother not to encourage him. Acts such as this may have turned on a secret revolutionary spirit in the young Han but they did not turn him from a purpose that persisted, a desire to be an artist and one that would reach the heights.

In 1908 his father relented in so far that he allowed his son to enter the Institute of Technology at Delft to study architecture. The young student in reality had little interest in buildings but used much of his time at the Institute to work away at his drawing and painting also on the History of Art coupled with the methods of the earlier masters.

In 1912 such was his progress and display of talent, that he was appointed Assistant at Delft in the course on Drawing and the History of Art. Here he had greater scope than before to press on with his own work. In 1913 he produced a water colour 'Interior of a Church' painted in the manner of the seventeenth-century Dutch Masters, which won for him the First Prize and Gold Medal at the Institute of Technology in Delft.

Just prior to this date he had made his first marriage. This was to Anna de Voogt by whom he had two children. Shortly after he moved to the Hague where for a time he was lionized by the social set; his drawings and paintings were in demand and he also found he could charge high fees for private and group lessons. An exhibition of biblical paintings in the Hague in 1922 was a sell-out. Weak traits in his character now became evident. He was unable to handle success. The adulation proved a corrosive factor.

He divorced Anna in 1928 and married the actress Johanna Theresia Oerlemans. Soon the praise of the critics for his work faded away and was replaced with more caustic comment. Van Meegeren had a streak in him that could not take rebuff and criticism. Here could have been the seed for his coming forgeries—works which he intended should make a fool of those who had derided him.

He decided to leave Holland and in 1932 moved to the South of France, first to Roquebrune and then to Nice. On his own admission he must have now had a further flush of legitimate success, building up a capital of some £15,000 by painting the portraits of rich American and British tourists. It was during a six- to seven-month stint in isolation between 1936 and 1937 at Roquebrune that he produced the 'Supper at Emmaus'.

Van Meegeren, brimming with contempt for the whole art world, collectors, critics and historians, set out to trap them. By training and possibly inclination he chose the early Dutch Masters. He produced competent fakes of Hals, de Hoogh and Terborgh. But he finally decided that it should be in the guise of Vermeer he would work for the great upset. The brilliant choice of subject he made was to present a Vermeer with religious content. Art historians and specialists were expecting the discovery of just such works. They had thought that Vermeer could have travelled to Italy and would have absorbed the influence of the Italian painters, notably the light and shade effects of Caravaggio. Some even thought the Dutch Master could have produced biblical pictures which could have hung ever since in the sanctuary of some secret religious society.

The first step was to obtain an old picture on canvas similar to that used by Vermeer and as far as possible the same date. In the case of the 'Supper at Emmaus', Van Meegeren purchased a version of the 'Resurrection of Lazarus'. The canvas was not the right proportion for his envisaged composition so he cut off a strip from one side and also remade the wooden stretcher to fit. Here he must have overlooked a clue which could be picked up. A canvas after a period of time that has been stretched with tacks tends to develop a deformation in the threads, a shallow looping occurs between the tacks on the edges of the stretcher. When the 'Supper at Emmaus' was thoroughly examined the looping appeared on the upper, lower and right hand edges but was absent on the left.

Before Van Meegeren started the new painting, most of the old painting had to be removed by the use of a brush and a cleansing agent, particular attention being paid to the areas containing white lead, as these could show up under an examination by radiography.

When he came to the actual production of his own painting Van Meegeren got round the difficulty of the long period of drying out for oil-bound colours by mixing the pigments with phenol and formaldehyde; the two chemicals that were used in the production of Bakelite, a hard synthetic material which had been developed in the United States in 1908. By slightly adjusting the amounts of these two chemicals, and the addition of synthetic lilac oil, Van Meegeren found that he could make the consistency of paint he sought. Heating up to about 100 degrees Centigrade for a period produced a film that was very hard and resistant to solvents which might have been used to assess the age of the paint. Another advantage was that as the paint dried with a slight loss of volume it tended to repeat the cracking in the remains of the

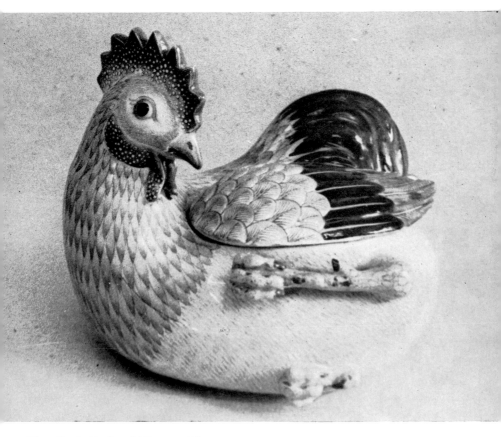

Plate 1. A Cockerel Tureen. The bird is enjoying a dust bath. Instead of being eighteenth century, it is twentieth century, and it is not Chinese Porcelain. Courtesy of Mr. Kiddell of Sotheby's.

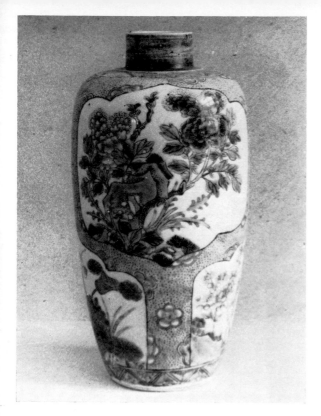

Plate 2. One of a pair of 'Famille Verte' Slender Oviform Vases. Made in the beginning of this century, in Paris. Courtesy of Mr. Kiddell of Sotheby's.

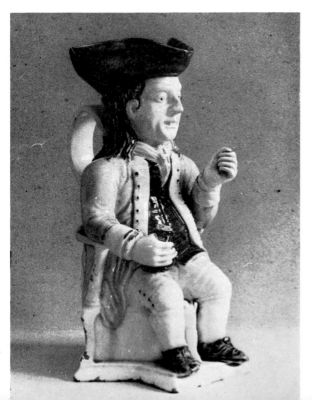

Plate 3. A Thin Man Toby. One of a series of good copies of Toby jugs; made prior to 1939, after a Ralph Wood original. Courtesy of Mr. Kiddell of Sotheby's.

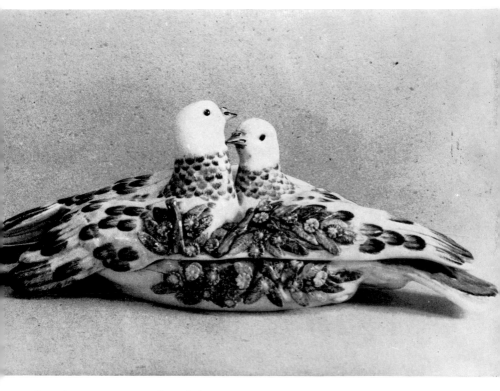

*Plate 4. Samson copy of a Chelsea
Double Pigeon Tureen and
Cover, carrying a spurious gold
anchor. Courtesy of Mr. Kiddell of
Sotheby's.*

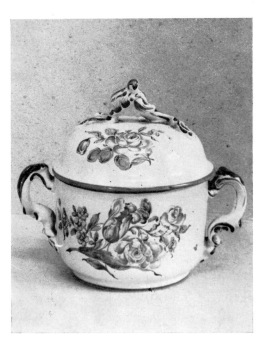

Plate 5. *Samson copy of a Marseilles Double-handled Bowl and Cover of unusual quality. Courtesy of Mr. Kiddell of Sotheby's.*

Plate 6. *Samson Marseilles Bowl showing factory mark and Samson's own mark. Courtesy of Mr. Kiddell of Sotheby's.*

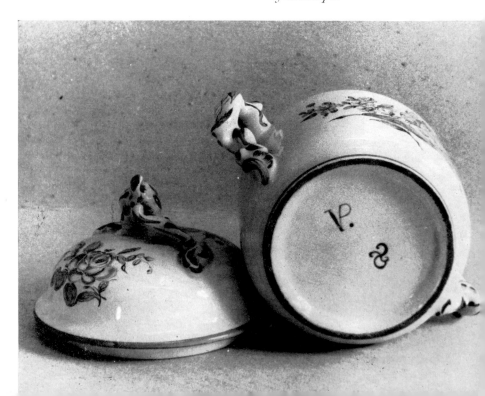

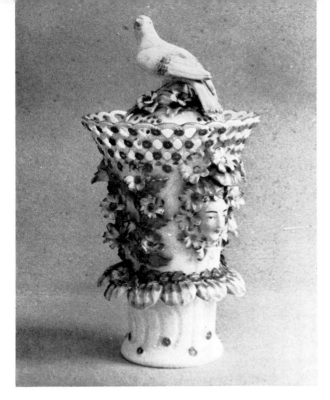

Plate 7. Samson copy of a Derby Frilled Beaker with Cover, amusingly marked with a gold anchor. Courtesy of Mr. Kiddell of Sotheby's.

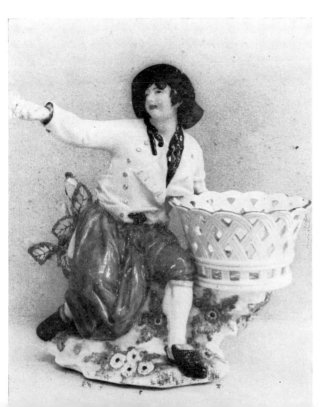

Plate 8. Samson copy of the well-known 'Chelsea Gardener with Basket'. Courtesy of Mr. Kiddell of Sotheby's.

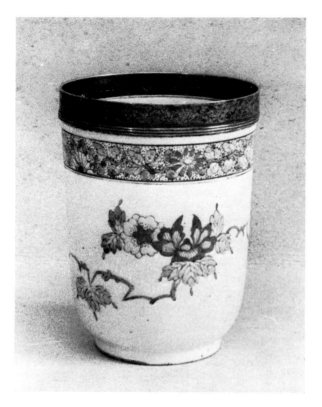

Plate 9. Samson copy of a Chantilly Kakiemon Decorated Beaker with Engraved Silver Mount. Probably inspired by the original in the Musee des Arts Decoratifs, Paris. Courtesy of Mr. Kiddell of Sotheby's.

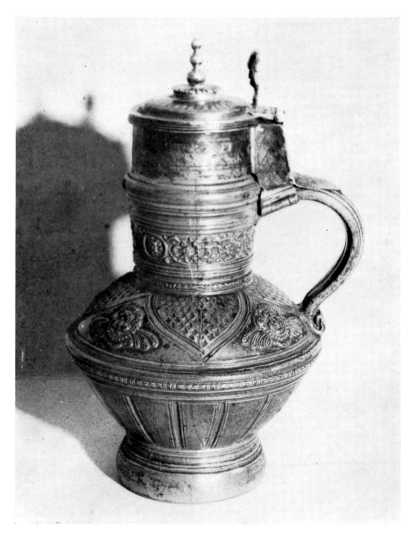

Plate 10. Raeren Stoneware Jug with Silver Gilt
Mounts, purporting to being 1580, actually produced
in 1885 by Hubert Schiffer. Courtesy of Mr. Kiddell
of Sotheby's.

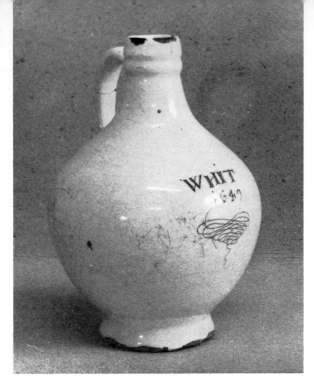

Plate *11. A Lambeth Delft Wine Bottle inscribed 'Whit 1649'; made in the early 1920s; too much crackle. Courtesy of Mr. Kiddell of Sotheby's.*

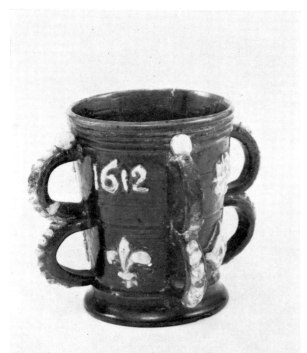

Plate *12. Castle Hedding-ham Tyg. Probably the work of Edward Bingham of Essex, c. 1870–1900. Courtesy of the Trustees of the British Museum.*

original paint on the old canvas. With a later forgery 'Washing of the Feet' Van Meegeren admitted he had raised the temperature too far and held it for too long. This had resulted in pitting which he had had to restore afterwards, the retouching being carried out in this case not with the synthetic medium but with oil.

With the 'Supper at Emmaus', the next step after the completion of the actual painting and hardening was to apply a layer of varnish which was solely intended as a mask when he came to fill the cracks with black ink. When this varnish was hard the canvas was rolled in several directions round a cylinder to produce a thorough minute cracking over the whole surface. The cracking complex had then to be filled with a dark substance. Van Meegeren chose black ink, again leaving a chink for uncovering the forgery. (Fine grime from the studio floor could have done the job as convincingly and its presence need not have aroused suspicion.) When the ink was dry the excess was washed off and the initial layer of varnish was removed with a mild solvent. The last touch was to brush on the final coat of varnish which was slightly tinted.

Van Meegeren, good scholar that he was, kept, with one exception, to pigments that could have been used by a seventeenth-century painter. From his studio afterwards were recovered specimens of burnt sienna, carbon black, gamboge, indigo, natural lapis lazuli (true ultramarine blue), raw and burnt umber, Venetian red, vermilion, white lead and yellow ochre. These were the colours that he kept for the 'Supper at Emmaus'. It is strange that in two later forgeries 'Woman taken in Adultery' and 'Woman reading music' small quantities of cobalt blue were found, a pigment that was not made until the early part of the nineteenth-century.

How was the issue of the 'Supper at Emmaus' engineered? Van Meegeren worked with a lawyer as middle man. At the start this gentleman brought the painting to the knowledge of Abraham Bredius, the doyen of European Art experts. Bredius, perhaps full with the theories on Vermeer's work that inspired Van Meegeren, readily gave the vital certificate of authenticity. This enabled confident approaches to be made for sale. In December 1937 the 'Supper at Emmaus' was bought for the Boymans Museum, Rotterdam, by the Rembrandt Society for £58,000 (close to £200,000 by today's value), the cost being shared between the Rembrandt Society and the State.

When the war came Van Meegeren returned to Holland and during the war years produced at least five more 'Vermeers' which brought his total take by forgery up to some £730,000 (close to £2 million by today's reckoning). When and how did the crunch come for him? By an unpredictable twist Han Van Meegeren was not arrested for issuing forgeries. He was seized by the police after the war as a collaborator. The post-hostilities Security and Investigation people had discovered what appeared to be a hitherto unknown Vermeer which had been bought by Hermann Goering and hidden away with other of his treasures in the Alt-Aussee salt mine in Austria. This painting was Van Meegeren's 'Woman taken in Adultery'. Assuming that it was a real Vermeer a national outcry arose as to why this treasure should have been sold to the hated enemy. After months of sifting records and following clues, inevitably the police back-tracked to Van Meegeren and he was arrested on 29 May 1945.

At first he denied all knowledge and then after a few weeks suddenly burst out with the then shattering comment, that he was no collaborator, he had not sold a national treasure, all he had done was to sell a fake, which he had in fact painted. At first there was disbelief. He painted a further example under supervision, 'Jesus among the Doctors'.

A full scale investigation both scientific and detecting was set up and gradually the fraud was laid bare. Even today more than two decades afterwards arguments still spring up in some quarters. It could be posed that without the denouement of the salt-mine find, would Van Meegeren have been discovered? It is of interest to note that the principal scientific investigator, the late Dr. Paul Coremans, gave the opinion that Van Meegeren was the greatest forger of all time. His preparatory work had been complete and intense. He had mastered the essence of Vermeer, his technique, colouring, and more had been able to transpose these methods from the oil technique of Vermeer to the use of a modern synthetic medium with its differences in handling. Han Van Meegeren in the end at his trial was given a year's imprisonment, but died before he could serve the sentence.

It should be remembered that the scientific investigation was not set in motion until after the confession of the forger. This very fact does set a poser for the collector. It is obviously quite impossible for the impedimenta of a full-scale laboratory examination to be given to every painting that appears. A retreat then has to be made into that undefinable area of the stylistic plus provenance. The latter can quite easily be questionable as it is open to forgery as much as the work in question. Looking at Van Meegeren's 'Supper at Emmaus' today it is quite a simple matter to feel that something is wrong with it; that there does not appear to be any bone in the left arm of the figure in front of the table to the right. A bright trained eye however must have spotted the deception way back in 1937; for one of Duveen's agents in Paris saw the canvas and cabled back to New York that it was a 'rotten fake'. But for every one spotting a forgery there must be an uncomfortably large number of people, yes experts too, who let it through their defences. Search and search again into the history, and where possible approach someone who can apply even quite rudimentary scientific examination.

In a lesser vein than Van Meegeren was Peter Thompson working in the nineteenth century. His flair was not only to fake but to invent completely the artist who was supposed to have produced the work. Thompson brought into being a Captain John Eyre. Of Thompson himself comparatively little is known. He lived in Regent's Park, London, and must have had some skill for architecture as he sent in designs for the competition for the new Houses of Parliament in 1835. But Thompson did provide a reasonable life story for his seventeenth-century artist.

Captain John Eyre was 'born' in Bakewell, Derbyshire, on 6

October 1604, supposedly a descendant of Simon Eyre the shoemaker Lord Mayor of London, a branch of whose family was known to have lived in that area. After being educated at Oxford it was indicated that he went with Prince Charles (Charles I) on his journeyings. There follows a convincing story of his Royalist activities until the trial of John Hampden, after which he switched to the support of the Roundheads. He 'met' Cromwell whom he 'painted'. He 'fought' with the Parliamentarians several times. At Marston Moor he was 'wounded' 'while charging at the head of his regiment'. He 'died' at Bakewell on 23 July 1644. After his 'death' some 300 specimens of his artistic work were found in his rooms.

Thompson made Eyre the producer mainly of descriptive architectural drawings. In style these leant to a degree on similar work by Wenceslaus Hollar. There were representations of the fortifications of London put up in 1643, sketches in pen and ink of monuments from London churches. The works were carried out on old paper with ink that appeared to have faded as might be expected with time. Many of them carried comments in an attempt at an early seventeenth-century script. Those that had representations of figures were the weakest. A portrait of the playwright Ben Jonson was a poor copy from a wall-painting in Shakespeare's house at Southwark.

To bring his 'artist' to the notice of the public, in 1852 Thompson brought out a series of etched facsimiles from the London fortifications drawings; these were priced between five and ten shillings and he had an impressive subscribers list that was topped by Prince Albert. In 1853 he contributed a letter to *Notes and Queries* that made reference to some work by Eyre that had a Shakespearean interest. The scheme did come under attack from some who doubted the authenticity of the original drawings; this caused at least one cancellation of an order for the series, from the Guildhall Library who had been on the subscription list. There are likely still to be 'Eyre's' floating around, in fact a drawing of 'Southwark Fair' has twice been brought to the British Museum as an authentic seventeenth-century work.

The Van Meegeren forgeries bore quite immaculately correct versions of Vermeer's signature. This kind of touch by the forger today will only take in the most innocent of collectors. A great name tagged on to a picture can have no more worth than the lot number in a sale. In the Middle Ages the painter worked first as a craftsman and to a large extent as anonymously as the rest. Even into the Renaissance the practice continued. Geniuses of the quality of Michelangelo and Raphael only on few occasions put their names to works. The adding of his signature to a picture by the artist probably started as an early form of copyright, an attempt to protect the work from plagiarism or an outright theft of property. Unfortunately with time the unscrupulous have taken advantage of the implication and played high and wide with the idea. One of the first artists to suffer from forged signatures or in this case monograms was Albrecht Dürer. The innovations and skill that he brought to engraving soon had the copyists at work and his famous AD mark was just too easy to add as a note of authenticity to the imitation.

Dürer published his series on the Apocalypse in 1498, and when he produced the third edition in 1511 he found it necessary to add a caution at the end telling would-be plagiarists that the Emperor Maximilian forbade anyone to copy the cuts or to sell fake prints of them within the limits of the Empire, under pain of confiscation of their goods and other possible punishments. Nine years previously in 1502 an edition of the Apocalypse had appeared under the initials I.V.F.; these copies had been made by a painter from Frankfurt, Hieronymus Greff. In 1512 one bold and impertinent character had had the effrontery to hawk faked Dürer prints complete with the AD monogram right outside the Rathaus in Nuremberg.

The best known of the Dürer plagiarists was an Italian, Marc Antonio Raimondi. Amongst other copies Raimondi produced on copper the 'Little Passion' and seventeen of the cuts of the 'Life of the Virgin' within a very short time of their publication by Dürer. Raimondi did not affix the AD to the prints of the 'Little Passion' but he did to those of the 'Life of the Virgin'.

With a copy of 'Adam and Eve' in 1504 he filled out the tablet exactly as Dürer had in the original, 'Albert Dvrer Noricos Faciebat 1504'. The Raimondi case is of interest because in his own right he was a considerable artist. Comparing his versions with Dürer's it can be seen how he brings in qualities of his own and makes them less faithful copies than those from other hands. It can only be imagined that his motive for the fraud was purely one of gain, to jump on a popular band-wagon. Dürer did attempt some form of remonstration through his patron Maximilian and the Imperial Ambassador to Venice but with what success is not clearly recorded.

Few artists can have attracted such a host of fakers and copyists as Dürer; Heller lists more than 300 people who worked *after* the Nuremberg genius. This includes Virgil Solis a talented engraver from Nuremberg who signed his copies VS. Another with talent was Hieronymus Wierx; most of his work in this field was done before he was twenty. His well-known version of the 'Knight, Death and the Rider' was done when he was only fifteen; this does not bear the AD monogram, just having the date 1564 in the tablet. Others who feigned the master's hand are J. C. Vischer, Ulrich Kraus, Martin Rota, Joh. van Goosen, Hieronymus and Lambert Hopfer and Erhard Schön.

The detection of a spurious print carried out a hundred years or more ago can be exceedingly difficult. The true story can be blurred by the addition of spurious or real collector's marks, and only occasionally are examples met with that have an unquestionable clean pedigree going back to the master. More recent attempts at forgery can founder on crude points such as a date mark similar to the Speed map mentioned earlier. Other tries can be picked out by analysis of the paper used. The case with the book forger Thomas James Wise (1859–1937) illustrates this point. Wise hit on the plan of forging First Editions of some of the works of well-known English writers including Byron, Ruskin and Wordsworth. He had a good run with this scheme and made himself a large sum until in the thirties scientific analysis disclosed the fact that the paper he was using was not what it should be. Tests showed that esparto grass and wood pulp had been used in the paper of these books supposedly published before 1861. Historical facts record that esparto was not used in paper until 1861 and chemically pulped wood fibre did not come in until 1874.

Confusion can also arise from a misunderstanding of the various printing methods. Relief processes such as woodcutting and wood-engraving by their method of inking and printing leave a negligible amount of upstanding ink. The woodcut is carried out on the plank grain and in general is much bolder than the engraving which is worked with fine tools on the end grain of woods such as box and cherry. The reverse of the relief print is the intaglio. Probably the best known example is the etching. With this manner the artist grounds his copper or zinc plate with a wax and resin mixture. Then using a needle he works his design to expose the metal. The plate is dipped into an acid or mordant bath so that the exposed lines are eaten out. The print is taken by forcing ink into the etched lines and wiping the surface of the plate. Slightly damped paper is laid on the plate and the whole passed through a press capable of exerting sufficient pressure to force the paper into the lines to pick up the ink. The resulting print has lines which are very slightly raised. These can sometimes be seen with the help of a raking light, or felt by the cautious touch of a fingertip. Another characteristic of an etching is that it can be printed with slight tone areas that are achieved by the artist purposely leaving delicate veils of ink on the plate during the surface wiping before making the print. As with paintings, spurious prints in general lack that feeling of rightness. Comparison with known examples in the great national collections will very often bring out the pretender.

Innocent copying, as has been mentioned, can bring confusion and illegitimate gain. Joseph Mallord William Turner was one of the most prolific British artists and in his time was greatly admired by that doyen of art critics and writers, John Ruskin. He with all good intent encouraged a number of artists to copy Turner's work to progress with their own. People such as Arthur Severn, H. B. Brabazon and William Hackstoun followed this advice and produced high quality replicas that have been accepted as Turner originals, until they have been brought to the British Museum and checked against the works from the Turner Bequest.

More mix-ups have probably been caused by fraudulent fiddling than the production of out-and-out fakes. This is partly because there are far more examples of the fiddling practice around than forgeries and partly because the fiddles generally have some essence of truth in their make-up.

The injudicious adding or subtracting of signatures goes back for several centuries. This may have started with the near inno-cent action of adding a genuine signature to an original painting by the artist represented by the signature. This came about probably by the demands of some of the earlier collectors who expected a signed work. But it has clearly branched out from this fairly harmless intention. Fashion here can play a part. In the early part of the nineteenth century Peter de Hoogh's work was held to have far greater quality than that of Vermeer, and thus Vermeer's distinctive picture 'The painter in his studio' bore the signature of Peter de Hoogh.

A picture of charm and quality may become a lodestone to the dealer if it bears some little known name. Collectors who sniff out their pieces with an art encyclopedia in one hand all too often shy away from a signature that is unknown or given little credit in the publication. It is a simple matter to erase the signature and to pass off the work as a lesser example by some well-known painter.

The addition of a signature today to an old painting has its drawbacks as it is difficult to age it into the earlier paint. It can be done after a cleaning and prior to the application of the varnish but it would be quite quickly exposed under scientific examin-ation. If it were put on top of the existing varnish it would certainly stand out too convincingly to fool any knowledgeable person, an examination with a strong glass should expose the deceit.

A device that does not really come under the heading of forgery proper is the horrible practice of slicing up. In the past many very large compositions were painted by quality artists. Today they are often too big to find hanging space. The philis-tine can blind himself to the original intention of the artist and cut up the picture into more convenient sizes. These may range from small landscapes from the background to heads and shoul-ders cut out from standing figures and transformed into portraits.

During the history of a painting it may have to suffer a long trail of maltreatment. Part of this may be just the effects of nature, time and day-to-day treatment. But sadly, all too often, man has to have a go. The attack may be from ideas of prudery; a nude may have a drapery inserted, a voluptuous seventeenth-century portrait of a lady may have a long thick curly lock of hair brought across in a judicious position. Figures and details can be completely painted out. Additions have been quite blatantly made, and if these have been done close to the period in which the original was painted they can be difficult first to detect and secondly to remove, as the two paint films may have been drying out together.

The constructor of the pastiche can often set hearts racing. He or she specializes in the building up of a work of art using fragments from either several pictures by another artist or by bringing together bits and pieces of works by several artists. There was one example that came to light in a small cottage in Ireland. This was lovingly protected in a fine wooden box and when it was brought out into the light gave the immediate impression of being early sixteenth-century German. On study it became more confusing as first it looked liked Lucas Cranach the elder and then Dürer. The support it was on was of the right date. What had happened was that some skilled hand contemporary with these masters had created a near convincing composition of details of both masters' works and had cleverly worked in characteristic features used very often by the painters.

Anachronisms can at times be the starting point for the discovery of a fake. These may appear in many forms. One of the most common is with costume, quite small details can be a give away. Interior decoration and furniture should be compared with authentic illustrations of the period that the painting is supposed to be from. Animal and plant forms should also be studied.

Recourse should always be made, when time allows, to the fullest possible perusal of documented and visual material concerning the artist. Many painters have left fairly comprehensive accounts of their work in the form of order and studio books,

3—FA * *

sketch books and other records. There are also increasingly available today definitive catalogues of the major painters and many lesser names. Hold in mind the case of poor Corot, for according to the number of works credited to him, said to be over 100,000 in America alone, he must have put in at least a 200-hour day.

3 _The Sculptor_

A CARVED OR MODELLED FIGURE IS IN MANY WAYS A FAR greater challenge for the forger than the production of a spurious painting or drawing. From being able to deceive on a flat plane he must be able to carry his skills convincingly into three dimensions. More than ever there is the demand upon him to capture and emulate the virtuosity of the man he is copying. The execution of a stone or wood figure, to be successful, calls for an all out aesthetic and physical effort; a pointing machine may provide some guide, but it can be no replacement for lack of talent with the chisel. The practitioner in clay or wax may be able to fall back on taking casts from originals to build up a pastiche; but, again, if he is to succeed in aping a master, his hands and tools must be able to impart the surging life that is present with the true work. The faker is faced not only with the technical difficulties of working his chosen material but, further, with giving it 'life' and veracity, from whatever position it is viewed.

In stone carving the principal materials that sculptors have used have been Carrara, Parian and Pentelic marbles (in America the Georgian marble), oölitic limestone, Hoptonwood stone, Purbeck marble, the grey and yellow sandstones, basalt and granite. For small figures in wood, box has been a favourite; whilst for larger works, timbers include ebony, walnut, oak, limewood and poplar. Bronze has been the most used material for casting, although there have been examples in lead. Terra cotta has been used for modelling and small objects have been carved from bone and ivory. Both stone and wood carvings have been polychromed and gilt, and for this treatment with wood there has generally been an underlying coat of gesso put on first as a ground not only for the gold and colours but also to receive stamped patterns, which were made whilst the gesso was still damp. Terra cotta has been left with its natural colour unglazed or has been painted and glazed. Bronze casts have been gilt, polished and treated with a wide variety of applied patinas.

When the first third-dimensional forgeries were made is impossible to state. There is certainly evidence that the ancient Greeks were at it and also the Romans. The appeal of the true Classic art had a very considerable resurgence during the Renaissance, particularly in Italy. There is the oft told story of Lorenzo de' Medici and Michelangelo. The young genius was at the time working under the patronage of Lorenzo, and in between producing sculptures to satisfy his master he did some work on his own including a version in marble of the 'Sleeping Cupid'. The little recumbent figure was executed in the Classic manner and when Lorenzo saw it, he admired the finish but not actually wanting it himself suggested to Michelangelo that if it were treated so as to appear antique it could have some market value. Accordingly the young sculptor is said to have buried the 'Sleeping Cupid' for a period in damp sour ground. This would affect the surface of the marble by staining so that it would appear to have considerable age. Lorenzo now sent the figure to Baldassare de Milanese, an art dealer in Rome, who promptly sold the 'aged' figure for two hundred gold ducats to Cardinal Riario of San Giorgio. All Michelangelo got from the dealer was thirty ducats. The upshot in the end was that the Cardinal got wind of the deception and forced Baldassare to return his money in full. Although the Cupid of Michelangelo has disappeared since his time, there have been a number of forgeries pertaining to be the 'Sleeping Cupid'.

A name which was to cause as great a reverberation in his own time as that of Van Meegeren, was Dossena. Immediately after the First World War the art scene, to a degree, was in chaos.

There was much selling and buying of treasures which created a fortuitous environment for the floating of fakes. In 1918 some sculptures of seeming superlative quality started to appear in Paris, and as these were sold others took their place. The origin of all these works was given as Italy; this fact set the rumours going as to where they could actually be coming from. Had the Vatican decided to part with some of its collection? Had some noble family been forced into ruin by the war and was now selling?

But it was none of these. The things were forgeries. But in basic truth the craftsman who made them was not at heart a forger. It was more the dealer to whom he sold his work and who then passed it off as original who was the forger.

The skilled hands which could as easily create the sculpture of the early Greeks and Romans, Gothic and Renaissance periods belonged to Alceo Dossena (1878–1937). A humble and in his own way self-effacing character, Dossena worked in a small craftroom alongside the river Tiber in Rome. He never laid any claim that his works were other than by himself. His inner thoughts are revealed by a comment he made, 'I was born in our times, but with the soul, taste and perception of other ages.' His misfortune seems to have been that he met an unscrupulous character who was to sell his work for a very large margin of profit. It is recorded how in 1916, on Christmas Eve, Dossena, who, at that time, was a soldier, was on leave in Rome and had with him a small figure of the Madonna in wood which he had carved. In a cafe he was introduced to the dealer Alfredo Fasoli who was at first taken in with the Madonna thinking that it was genuinely old and might have been picked up somewhere by the soldier in his duties. He paid Dossena 100 lire, and it was only when he later examined the carving thoroughly that he found out it was in fact a modern work. But Fasoli was enough of an expert to realize the talent that must be in Dossena.

When accident brought them together once more, Fasoli had his plans laid. He persuaded the sculptor to bring out further examples and to apply devices that would give them a convincing appearance of age. So from the small workshop began to come forth almost a spate of carved stone, wood and terra cotta figures. Even by the most vicious standards of profit Fasoli was at the top. Dossena produced on order for the dealer an 'Early Renaissance' tomb in the style of Mino da Fiesole. This was ultimately disposed of for 6,000,000 lire and all the share that Dossena received was 25,000 lire. For several years, for the dealers and middlemen, the fun must have been fast and furious. Provenances for the emerging masterpieces, certificates of authenticity, invented collections where they had supposedly been were all forthcoming. Much gold for the inner circle flowed. But the procreator was in innocence. As far as he was concerned, when the works left his studio they did so under his name. However, after a while Dossena began to hear whispers of enormous prices some people were paying for his works. About the same time he found himself short of money and tried unsuccessfully to raise some in advance on the next batch for the dealers. The harsh rebuff he received triggered off the exposé then made by Dossena himself.

At first the world would have none of it. How could someone of such a lowly origin as Dossena have wrought such masterpieces? Critics, connoisseurs, museum directors had all been fooled. They now thought up every device they could to discredit Dossena's admission. Attempts were made to establish that he had not really created, only copied; but no one ever brought forward a specimen from the past that Dossena could have seen. Convincing evidence that he could really do the work was given by Dossena when he allowed himself to be filmed whilst actually modelling. In many ways his sheer virtuosity in the handling of his materials and in the ease with which he could bring into being examples from many different periods presented the art world with a trying problem. Here was a unique hand that could seemingly flit from style to style without having to slavishly copy or resort to other research. His end was sad. After trying to bring fraud actions against Fasoli and another dealer, he was himself attacked by Fasoli as a political agitator. His last days were spent in a Rome pauper's hospital.

Classical period sculpture has a great attraction for many. Museums and galleries need examples if their collections are to be complete. Collectors will bid keenly for objects from the early

Greek and Roman times. Dossena's work, via the middlemen, had taken in not only private collectors but also many major gallery and museum directors and their experts. The Boston Museum of Fine Arts had bought Dossena's 'Sarcophagus by Mino da Fiesole'. The Metropolitan Museum in New York had his 'Greek Goddess'.

This latter museum, on 16 February 1923, bought what was accepted as a fine example of Greek art at its height. The seller was a dealer in Paris; the piece a bronze horse that dated from about 480 to 470 B.C. Learned writing backed the appearance of the horse and its authenticity was never questioned either stylistically or from the technical production of the cast. For some thirty-eight years it stood in splendour surrounded by the admiration of countless eyes. Thousands of plaster cast copies of the animal were sold. In 1961 suddenly doubt was raised about the method of casting used to make the horse. Visual examination showed two holes: one in the mane, and the other in the forelock. If that in the mane was meant for harness, it seemed to be in the wrong place, because the bridle straps should fasten right behind the ears. There was some perplexity about the reason for the hole in the forelock. One theory was that a supposed forger (in doing his homework) might have examined the statues on the Acropolis. Here both those of horses and female korai have holes in the tops of their heads. It could have been assumed that such holes were put there to carry some sort of ceremonial plumes, and so a hole for such a purpose might have been included in the horse, it was thought. Actually what the holes in the heads of the sculptures on the Acropolis are really for is to hold a bronze or iron spike to prevent the pigeons from perching.

For years the horse had been considered genuine, and these doubts caused quite an upheaval. A bronze founder in Brooklyn was brought in, and he put forward the idea that the horse could have been cast with a core of sand and clay that was held in position by pieces of iron wire while the molten bronze was poured. If there had been a forger, he would then have hidden the ends of the iron wires by cutting them back and filling the small surface holes with bronze plugs. This theory appeared to be upheld by the use of a magnet which traced the direction of these internal iron wires. Their presence was substantiated by radiography.

The possibility of a forgery now did seem likely, and for a number of years the little horse was looked upon as a fake by the Metropolitan Museum, although there were still those who thought otherwise. And indeed subsequent examination of the composition of the bronze alloy and other related factors has suggested that the horse is after all genuine. However a final conclusion has yet to be arrived at. These contradictions often seem to appear with forgeries that hit the top head-lines, as for instance with Van Meegeren and with the following account.

A coloured wax bust of 'Flora', supposedly an original work by Leonardo da Vinci, was bought for the Berlin Museum in 1909. The reason for the dismay and confusion that centres round this object for some collectors could be that here even more than with Van Meegeren, experts have joined battle from diametrically opposite view-points. First-rate scholars presented conflicting opinions. On one side was lined up those who were convinced that the bust were an original Da Vinci; these included Wilhelm von Bode, Edmund Hildebrandt, and the art critic from the *Berliner Tageblatt*, Adolph Donath. One of those most vociferous against the work and declaring that it was a fake was Gustav Pauli of the Kunsthalle, Hamburg. He was certain that the bust was stylistically out of period and more in line with figures modelled of Queen Victoria. Then a writer to *The Times* put forward the idea that the work had been modelled by Richard Cockle Lucas (1800–83), a little known English sculptor. The son of Lucas was still living at the time and he said that he could recall having helped his father with the bust. The model had been made from a painting of the Leonardo School that a dealer had brought to them and asked for a copy to be made. In 1910 the position became more fogged still when an English art historian, E. V. Lucas, referred to the bust as the work of his namesake sculptor and then after a fourteen-year gap sent his opinion to *The Times* that after all the 'Flora' was the authentic work of Da Vinci.

Laboratory tests were made on tiny fragments of paint which

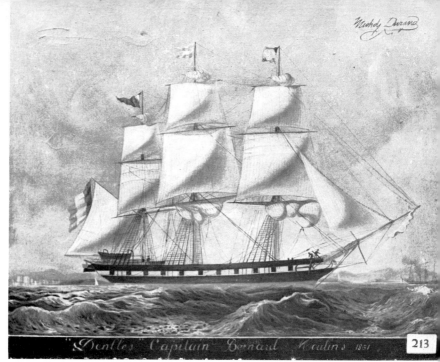

213

Plate 13. A modern painting in acrylic, from Spain,
with a false appearance of age.

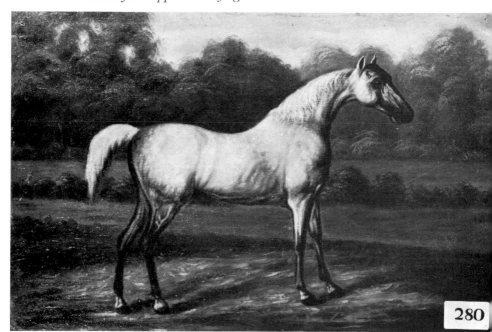

280

Plate 14. A spurious horse painting, carried out in
acrylic, from Spain. With acrylic colours a slight
rubbery feel is generally a lasting feature of the paint
film.

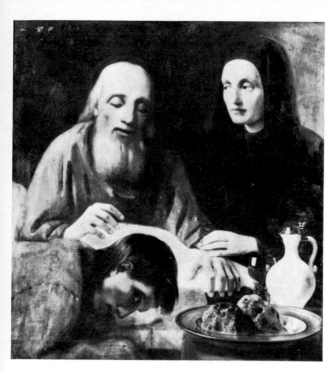

Plate 15. The Blessing of Jacob—Van Meegeren. Courtesy of the Institut Royal du Patrimoine Artistique, Brussels.

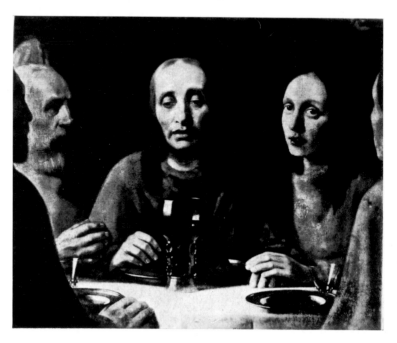

Plate 16. The Last Supper, detail—Van Meegeren. Courtesy of the Institut Royal du Patrimoine Artistique, Brussels.

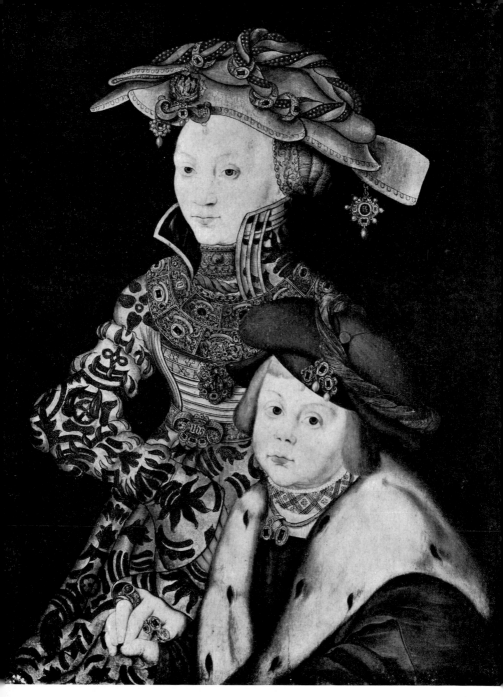

Plate 17. A fake of a Lucas Cranach by Franz Wolfgang Rohrich. By courtesy of the Doerner Institute, Munich.

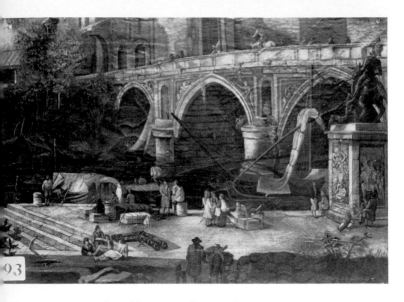

Plate *18*. *A pseudo period scene, painted with acrylic colours, and emanating from a studio in Spain.*

Plate *19*. *The making of deceptive copies of paintings is as old in China as the T'ang Dynasty (A.D. 618–908). Their purpose was to preserve or reproduce the compositions and styles of famous painters. The original seals and signatures would also be copied as a matter of course. Courtesy of the Trustees of the British Museum.*

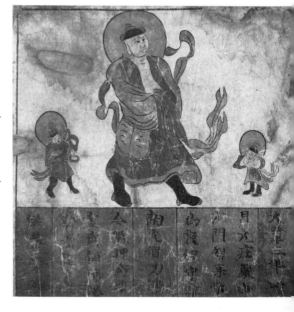

had been taken from the bust. Micro-chemical analysis brought out that there were traces of archil present; this is a dye that is prepared from lichen. Although archil is a colour that was used in earlier centuries, this fact alone could not establish that the 'Flora' was genuine; for a good forger could quite easily make up this colour. This was underlined when one expert, Theodor von Frimmel, in 1911, pointed out that anyway archil was still obtainable well after the end of the sixteenth century.

After this, to a degree matters became still more complicated and chaotic. Augusto Jandolo announced that another 'Flora' had turned up; but this time in marble not wax. It had been bought by an art dealer, Alfredo Barsanti, for 50 lire. He had then delighted himself by selling it to the Museum of Fine Arts in Boston for 48,000 lire. The bust reposed there in splendour, being described by L. D. Caskey as one of the great treasures of the collection.

Easy success must have gone to the head of Barsanti as he found and bought yet another 'Flora' in Florence; this one being accredited to Verrocchio, who had been the master of Leonardo da Vinci. Barsanti had paid 2,000 lire for this bust but found himself in the position of not being able to resell it, as leading experts said it was a rather poor fake. Barsanti then, perhaps unwisely, set about cleaning the 'Flora'. But he was fortunate and must have restored the bust to something like its original state; for shortly afterwards the Italian art historian Ruddioro Schiff gave his opinion that it was in fact quite authentic. It was finally bought by Lord Duveen despite further conflicting opinions.

When the collector witnesses such extraordinarily perplexing contradictions that surround the first 'Flora', the buying of art and antiques seems to take on the ring of the old fairground adage that goes something like 'You pays your money and you takes your chance'.

The field of money or rather coins and medals has for a long time been an enticement to the forger, and today there are certainly a great many examples of dubious origin in circulation. The concern here is with forgeries from the past but it is worth mentioning that there have been not very long ago many attempts to pass off current coinage especially where the bullion value is close to that on the face of the coin. Examples of this have been British gold sovereign replicas that have originated from Italy.

Coin and medal collecting really started in the sixteenth century, and ever since then the market has been plagued with fakes and copies. Simple casts from medals and coins, both false and genuine, have been made in very large numbers. When these have been produced by the latest type of pressure-casting they can easily trap the collector and even at times get past the trained eye.

In the field of medals come those two bright lads, William Smith and Charles Eaton. In the latter half of the nineteenth century they were spinning out a chancy living mudraking in between tides in the Pool of London. They had witnessed another such as themselves uncover a collection of small pilgrim medals; objects that had originally been made for people visiting the Holy Land. They soon found out that these would fetch a good price with dealers and collectors. The two men gave up their arduous and messy work to turn to satisfying what was an obviously ready market for 'pilgrim medals'. In a small house in Rosemary Street near the Tower of London they set up what, for a short time, was to be a highly profitable business. From this address poured forth thousands of medals made of lead, or so-called 'cock metal', an alloy of lead and copper. These purported to be from the Middle Ages. Their methods were simple. After the medals had been made they were carefully taken down to the river's edge during the hours of darkness and deposited in the mud. The next day the fakes would be disinterred, probably with a certain amount of show, and another batch would be on the way to the unwary. It is likely that the regular supplies may have aroused suspicion, for some dealers started to ask questions. An investigation followed, but the products of Smith and Eaton were cleared on the evidence of leading experts in the field. So back they went into full production. But in the end the sheer lack of knowledge on their part was to trap them. A scholar showed that there was something drastically wrong with some of the inscriptions. These were just nonsense; others pertained to be in Arabic. It was the latter which was one of the main mistakes that caught them out. The medals were supposedly from the eleventh century. The expert pointed out that Arabic was not known until two centuries later in Europe. More than this, Smith and Eaton carelessly included a number of anachronisms in their depictions of armour and other features. These rather ludicrous little fakes can still be come across. Known as 'Billies and Charleys', they may be openly sold as such or they may still be catching a few who buy without taking a careful look.

It was a good thing for Billy and Charley that they did not live actually in the Middle Ages, for in those times the law was somewhat more severe. Criminal records show that the making of false matrices could carry the penalty of death, and banishing and branding were not uncommon. The Chevalier Bouchard de Poissy was fined 4,000 livres and banished from Paris in 1356 for forging a seal. Modern forgeries in this line are not cut intaglio as were the originals, but are cast from impressions. Inevitably many of the impressions from which the fakes are made are already worn and lacking in detail, and this is of course evident in the cast. With the original the deepest part of the intaglio which is most protected retains the detail, whereas the opposite is true for the impression which has this part upstanding and so open to wear.

Towards the end of the nineteenth century the authorities of the Louvre, in Paris, were taken in by a remarkable piece of deception. Somewhat precipitously 200,000 francs was paid out for a unique and strange gold object. This was known, and still is, as the 'Tiara of Saitaphernes'. In many ways, here was a triumph of craftsmanship for the forger. The tiara had been presented with a well-sounding provenance and had a quality of workmanship that for a long time convinced the Louvre of its authenticity. It was modelled in the shape of head-gear of the early Persian kings which had later been copied as the format of that to be worn by the popes, and it was decorated largely with highly skilled repoussé work.

The advent of this curiosity came in February 1896 with the Russian dealer Schapschelle Hochman appearing in Vienna with a collection of antiquities which he claimed had been excavated from the ruins of an early Greek settlement at Olbia on the Black

Sea. Part of the fabricated history behind the object was, that in the second century B.C., the people had presented Saitaphernes, the Scythian king, with the tiara; there was a citation between the decorations which ran 'The Senate and People of Olbia to the Great Invincible Saitaphernes'. The tiara with other pieces that included necklaces, ear-rings and horn-books were offered to the Imperial Court Museum in Vienna through the agents Vogel and Szymanski. The connoisseurs Count Wilczek and Baron Nathaniel Rothschild were impressed particularly by the tiara and were sure it was genuine; as too was Otto Bendorf, a leading archaeologist, who said that here was a fine piece of work by a craftsman from pre-Christian times. His advice to the two collectors was that it should be bought for the Museum collections. The main distrust seems to have been from the Director of the Museum, Bruno Buchner. One of the contentions he raised was that it seemed strange that damaged areas were confined to parts free from decoration whilst delicate repoussé work remained undamaged. This seemed a conclusive argument against the authenticity of the piece which was supposed to be some two thousand years old and to have been buried for all those hundreds of years since. Buchner advised against the purchase.

In March the two agents travelled to Paris again to try their luck. This time it held. To a degree there was a parallel with the 'Supper at Emmaus' by Van Meegeren. Here was a unique piece of work that had to many intents and purposes quite rightful provenance and quality. It is interesting to note that, as with the Van Meegeren, a very respectable price was being asked—a device that must surely have helped greatly with the issue of many forgeries. If the passer of fakes has the nerve to price up his product, there seems to be a quirk in human nature that almost wills some people to equate inflated value with authenticity.

In Paris the tiara was examined by two experts from the Louvre, M. A. Kaempfen and M. E. Héron de Villefosse, who were both satisfied that it was genuine. They knew that other finds of the period from Olbia, according to reports, were stylistically similar, although, as these were in Russia, there was no way of making a comparison. Funds for the purchase of this splendid object were supplied by two private persons, and the sale appears to have been consummated with a degree of speed, perhaps spurred on by the thought that if it were delayed the Russian authorities might raise objections to this great rarity being allowed to leave the country for good.

On the somewhat suitable date of 1 April 1896 the tiara was put on display in the Louvre. But soon the doubting voices from various quarters began to sound off. One of the first was Professor Wesselovsky from the University of St. Petersburg. He proclaimed that the tiara was a modern fake and similar to many that had got themselves into Russian and Polish museums. If he had spoken a little earlier the Louvre authorities would have done well to listen, as Wesselovsky was in the position of being able to base his judgement on comparison with other Russian antiquities of these earlier periods. The fresh new tone of the gold worried the German archaeologist Adolf Furtwängler from Munich. The slight warm tone that was consonant with excavated gold antiquities was missing. He further started to draw attention to certain anachronisms in the handling of the figures, their clothing and, more so, to the anatomy. Here had been a stumbling block for the forger. Indeed this same point has defeated others. It is one thing to be a skilled metal-smith, carver or painter, but it is quite another to be able to slip into the guise of a craftsman from a particular period and to simulate convincingly the total product. The forger must be able to use his tools in the manner in which they would have been handled, also to reproduce surface finishes right for the period. On top of this he must somehow be able to re-create the whole aesthetic feel of that time. This is for him the toughest part because the manner and the 'feel' of a particular period or artist or craftsman have undefinable qualities which can only be sensed and appreciated after intensive study.

Furtwängler was joined in his theories by Professor Stern of the Odessa Museum in August 1896. On the other side, one of the Keepers from the Hermitage in St. Petersburg came out with the opinion that the tiara was genuine, although later he was to retract. As with the 'Flora' battle of 'it's a fake, it's genuine', it went on for several years, pundits not only voicing their opinions but committing them to paper. Then came an exposé almost in the manner of Dossena. In 1903, from Odessa word was sent that Israel Ruchomovsky, a goldsmith, admitted that he had made the tiara between 1895 and 1896 for a client who was to remain nameless. The pattern of many other fake exposures was then repeated. Ruchomovsky was at first disbelieved, then lauded as one who had been able to discredit and bring mockery on the experts who had been caught out, and lastly discarded as a cheat. But, as with Dossena, more of the blame should be put on the dealer than the maker; for Schapschelle Hochman and his brother had been commissioning 'antiquities' from Ruchomovsky in the 1890s; in fact, in 1897 the Director of the Odessa Museum had warned of this practice.

Israel Ruchomovsky had been born in Mosyr in 1860 and had moved to Odessa in 1892. The interesting point is that according to records he taught himself the difficult craft of gold- and silver-work and although it was shown later that much of the motifs and decoration on the tiara was taken from known sources, a fact which Ruchomovsky admitted, and there were stylistic faults and other deficiencies, there was that about the work that showed clearly that the craftsman who had made it was in his own right a very considerable artist.

The upshot of the admission was that Ruchomovsky went to Paris to demonstrate his claim to being the originator. Under oral examination he satisfied many of the objections against his assertions by exact descriptions of how the tiara had been made. But some at the Louvre were still not quite sure and he was asked to make a replica of part of the tiara without having the original to work from. Although it is not quite certain which section he made, Ruchomovsky's skill was obviously evident and the disbelief was quelled.

The case undoubtedly sent an unpleasant shiver through sections of the art world and threw up waves of doubt and questions in the minds of the public. As with later 'high grade' deceptions, more and more the layman wants to know just what art prices are about. Provenances are given careful scrutiny and certificates from past experts are losing credit value. The oft recurring query is, are the makers of fakes in the category of the tiara and others of such a quality as clever and full of talent as the main stream masters? This is a difficult question to answer fully and satisfactorily. In the case of Ruchomovsky it is obvious that his skill as a metal-smith was well up to many of the great ones before him, yet on his own admission the articles he made were leaning on the creative designs of others before him. He, Ruchomovsky, was akin to many another forger; technically there was skill in abundance, but original creativeness was lacking. Dossena and Van Meegeren are apart to an extent, in that, they were not copyists. Dossena appears to have been an innocent and one who must have had a genuine source talent. Van Meegeren, as was seen in the preceding chapter, made a careful and scheming attack but from an original angle.

4 *The Craftsman*

THE THINGS THAT WE SIT ON, SIT AT, EAT AND DRINK
with, store articles in and cosset our lives with have for
hundreds of years attracted the finest talent in design and
craftsmanship. Needless to say they have also attracted excellent talent from the out and out forger and innocent copyist.
As mass production of everyday items tends to remove a
desire or a possibility for the practice of craftsmanship so a
situation is being created in which there is a growing demand
of already astonishing dimensions for objects of beauty and
interest which have been produced in the past by the skilled
from fine materials.

As with paintings and sculpture, so with various categories
of craftsmen's work, there can be pastiches. Perhaps with
furniture a more descriptive word for the treatment is marriage. The ceremonies that have taken place in the past and are
still being enacted compass a wide field. Fragments from
several genuine broken pieces are built up to form a new one.
Old timbers are in demand for the trade, as it is well-nigh
impossible to age new wood.

The safest preparatory course for the embryo collector of
domestic necessities is to spend as liberal an amount of time as
possible in the galleries or museums to study proven pieces of
quality from the past. Endeavour to learn off visually the looks
of the various woods that have been used either in a solid

form or as veneers and inlays. Observe the way in which master craftsmen have used the grain and qualities of the wood. See how the patina of time and care differs so vastly from the glitter-glare of some present day polishes. That wonderful sheen of old oak is the result largely of good honest beeswax and turpentine and plenty of rubbing which also imparts that feeling of gentle ageing. Hard edges have been softened, slowly the years have altered the tones of the timbers to leave them with an incomparable mellow look. This last is the most frustrating for the forger, for it can never quite be approached.

The ageing of new wood and parts of old timber that have been reworked can call for much ingenuity. The judging of the correct dried-in tone needs experience. Various staining agents have been used. Walnut-juice has been in favour also permanganate of potash. Nitric acid has been employed but this can produce after-effects, in that, if it is overdone, the immediate surface of the wood can start to distintegrate as it is literally burnt away by the acid. Freshly carved forms are difficult to stain effectively, for the colour can run too freely into the details and upstanding parts be left too light. Decorative carving should always be examined carefully not only for tonal variation but also in the deepest parts of the cutting; if the example is genuine the accretions of wax and grime should be hard. Wax to a degree dries like oil-colours; that is, after a quite short time it is touch-dry but it will take a very long time to really harden right out. Therefore if the residual wax at the bottom of carved crevices is still soft to the touch of a needle, the piece should be given a very long look.

Too much reliance is put on the wood-worm and his little tunnels. For some the mere fact that there are holes in the wood will guarantee age. But this is not a reliable premise because the little brutes will devour new wood with just as much relish. One of the reasons they appear all too often to have a go at old pieces of furniture is because ancient cracked timbers and opening joints allow for plentiful collections of dust and grime which provide one of the favourite environments wherein this pest can breed. Many people probably associate furniture forgers with shot-guns. So many times it has been put forward that this is the favourite tool for stimulating the holes of wood-worms. Apart from the fact that a shot-gun charge lays a fairly easily recognizable pattern, it would be a relatively easy task to pick out the remnants of the lead shot from the holes. There are however quite sophisticated mechanical tools for making spurious worm holes. But such holes will not be very deep and if in doubt about an article the holes can be quite simply tested.

Needless to say, if an assumed genuine article should exhibit longitudinally open worm tunnels, this would be a warning note; for it would imply that the original craftsman had made up the piece from wood already worm-eaten. This could be a rare possibility but is so unlikely that it might almost be disregarded. Genuine old worm-eaten timber should only have the round exit holes. To a degree open wood-worm tunnels can be filled with commercial 'plastic' woods or wax pastes but these can generally be picked up by slight surface variations. If this is suspected a raking light will often show them up clearly.

The usage of natural wear is another pointer to watch for. The bars on tables after a hundred years or more have smooth depressions worn in them. The arms of chairs all tend to have a slight lowering of the surface from the contact they have received. These can be quite subtle points but give-aways and fairly trying problems for the forger to simulate. This conveying the appearance of age to recently fabricated furniture is attempted in a variety of ways. It can be done by the use of abrasives; bruising can be induced by heavy rubbing with iron bars along the edges or even bashing with hard wooden mallets. Water-staining can easily be done. But even if the greatest care is used the final aged surface polish will very often be the tell-tale. Over-waxing can cover much, but this in itself can be generally detected with a finger nail. One trick which is very difficult at times to see through is the after treatment of lavish waxing; with this the final gesture is to polish the surface hard with a piece of cotton wool slightly moistened with a gentle solvent such as turpentine substitute. This will tend to remove excess wax and if the polishing is kept up for some time bring into being that illusive sheen of true patina.

Outside of museums and some private collections a truly original piece of furniture is becoming somewhat of a rarity. The large majority will to a lesser or greater degree have suffered somewhere during their history. It may be quite simple repairs necessary from usage; it may be slight restoration of damaged or lost areas. Here perhaps the difference between restoration and conservation could be clarified. For the really valuable and rare piece it is the latter treatment that should be given. The conservator works quite literally to consolidate and hold on to what is left, putting in as little new work as is possible. All too often the restorer overdoes his brief and adds more than is required.

Around about the 1850s furniture fiddlers discovered the super gloss treatment of French polish. This is slick varnish that is prepared from shellac and a suitable solvent, it can range in tone from a deep warm brown to a pale lemon brown depending on the type of shellac used. For the connoisseur the most distressing feature about it is that an overall gloss is achieved which will cover up too much. The finish has little feel with it. Unfortunately many fine pieces were stripped of their exquisite patinas and then treated to a uniform layer of French polish.

Another feature to look for in suspect articles is any sign that the timbers may have been used for other purposes than the actual building of the piece. These can range from old nail or screw holes that have been filled in to tonal differences between pieces of wood. The latter could be natural but if it is combined with a tint difference and obvious grain variety it is probably an addition.

Returning to the marriage theme there are too many articles of seemingly fine furniture about that are in truth assemblages of bits and pieces. These components may in fact have considerable age themselves, they may be antique but they will not necessarily all be from the same period, country or design fashion of the time. The main defence with piecemeal furniture is a thorough study of periods, with special attention to the types of wood used, the types of decorative detail, carving and construction that were in current usage. The faker on the whole does his homework well and is adept at disguising his make-believes.

However anachronisms do creep in. The overall style of one period may be found with a decorative treatment that is from another. This can occur with inlaid work where patterns are out of time for the supposed age of the piece. There have been examples of the application of heavy inlay work to moderately plain good furniture right for its time. This may be the work of an over zealous but ignorant faker or sadly it may have been specially carried out as an order from a customer. This decoration for decoration's sake, in many cases reached its zenith in the Victorian times when it appeared to be a sin to leave any plain simple areas at all. All too often, as well, the carving and applied design work was over-lavish and crude in execution.

Alteration of use or intent if carried out with skill can at the best be misleading and at worst can dupe the collector unless he has thoroughly grounded himself in styles and designs from the various periods. The numbers of chest-of-drawers that have been switched to desks, and tallboys that have been truncated are legion. Close examination of jointing might show up the deceptions but if it has been really well done it can get past. The usual glues of past cabinet-makers were generally of the hoof variety or rabbit-skin. But the presence of modern synthetics would not necessarily point to a fake as the adhesive could have been used for a legitimate mend. Machine made screws and nails should be watched for, although again they need not necessarily be conclusive as they could have been put into a perfectly genuine piece as a slipshod repair.

Today there is an increasing flow of reproduction furniture to satisfy a seemingly insatiable demand to be surrounded if not with age by the suggestion of age. This can range from the really frightful 'antiqued' objects, with their conglomeration of motifs and revolting sprayed on 'age' shading to highly accomplished and skilled products that will be very close to the period they intend. All right at the moment as they will be made of easily identifiable new wood and metal fittings. But what will the position be for the less than astute collectors of 2070?. The pieces will by then have accumulated their own ageing, and they may also have been tinkered with on the way. Modern metal fittings which could be an obvious give-away could have been removed and replaced with older hand-made versions from the workshop scrap-heap.

The smart forger is not only an accomplished craftsman but he is also an observant scoundrel who keeps his eyes wide open for trends in the buying public's taste. One rising fashion is for collecting musical instruments. Unhappily for many musicians these are being bought not necessarily to be played but rather as status investments. Prices in the auction rooms have been rising and the forger has registered the fact. In the 1930s a fair number of fake violins were coming out of Czechoslovakia, many of them brazenly carrying labels which read 'Antonius Stradivarius Cremonensis'. Since the war others purporting to be genuine 'Strads' have been seeping on to the market from workshops in France and Eastern Germany. Investment collecting has to an extent assisted the forger of musical instruments. For in earlier times he would not only have needed to produce a convincing looking instrument but also he would have needed to be sufficient master of his intent to be sure that his 'masterpiece' would play correctly and sound correct. Not only would the eye need to be deceived but at the same time the ear must be assured. Today, for many, visual satisfaction would be sufficient.

The field of ceramics has not been neglected by the forger; his wares have been spread right across the board. When there is a demand he is there to fill it. In 1971 the Turkish police pulled in a man on a charge of faking pottery of the Anatolian Neolithic period from some 7,000 to 8,000 years ago. Over the past decade examples of this ware have been purchased by not only private collectors in Europe and the United States of America but also by leading museums, including the Ashmolean at Oxford, the British Museum and the Metropolitan Museum of Art in New York. They were all under the impression that they were buying genuine objects dug up from the prehistoric settlement and cemetery at Hacilar in south-west Turkey. This site was discovered in 1956 and excavated from 1957 to 1960. It was known that the site had been looted and it was thought that the objects coming up for sale were from this source, and had been illegally smuggled out of Turkey. Some may have been but somewhere along the supply line there had been an infiltration of what were to turn out to be fakes. Suspicion was aroused and a number of the pieces were tested for age using the thermoluminescent dating technique mentioned in Chapter Seven. Some sixty-six pieces were tested, that included primitive painted bowls, figures and anthropomorphic vases. The result came up that out of this total forty-eight pieces were modern fakes. Further the clays were examined by chemical analysis which pointed to the fact that they had a composition which was different from that of the authentic Hacilar pottery. Another piece of evidence was that a number of the fakes had a white crusting that was soft and non-calcareous which could hardly have been acquired naturally in the district.

When encouraged the forger will advance almost into the field of total mass production. Not only this, but he will not necessarily go for the high priced items but will be content to bring out a large number of quite humble objects. An instance of this occurred in Italy with Roman terra-cotta lamps. A huge collection of these had been assembled by the Italian antiquary Giovanni Battista Passeri, who lived between 1694 and 1780. This collection by Passeri, which was one of the world's most comprehensive and largest was housed in the Pesaro Museum. About fifty years ago doubts were raised as to the authenticity of these objects. Research and examination by specialists showed that the hitherto respected collection was in reality one of the largest accumulations of fakes. Nearly all the best specimens were spurious. One lamp in particular held a clue which had been overlooked by earlier authorities. This was one which was made in the form of a bull's head. Earlier opinions had stressed that lamps made to this design had been dedicated to the goddess Artemis Taurobolos. The forger in this case following through his researches had duly put an inscription on the horns to this lady but had neglected his spelling.

There has been the case where experts had actually gone to

considerable lengths to 'prove' a fake to be genuine. An early Christian lamp came to light which was in the shape of a fish and had on one side Christ's monogram, represented by inter- woven Greek letters and on the other a cross. Theorists put forward the idea that the whole stood for a symbol of Christ. The forger even went further and had actually put a smaller fish in the mouth of the larger. This was explained by one scholar in an effort to further substantiate the authenticity of the fake as being inspired by the New Testament words 'I will make you to become fishers of men'. It is possible that the forger was not a good enough theologian to have thought this out for himself. At any rate his attractive little fish lamp must have been produced in quite some numbers for it turned up in several museums, including the Berlin Museum, which bought two.

Another favourite with forgers using terra-cotta has been the production of small statuettes. The best publicized of these efforts has probably been the so-called Tanagras which were produced in the style of the late fourth and third centuries B.C. Many of these statuettes were cast from high quality originals, and if a dubious example can be compared with its original it is normally possible to point to the fake. The reason for this is that the forgery will be slightly smaller owing to the fact that the terra-cotta will shrink during the drying-out and the firing in the kiln.

Forgers working on ancient pottery examples have at times built up pastiches from genuine fragments, although in these cases their skill as restorers is not matched by their knowledge of early designs and the products have no ring of truth about their appearance. Genuine potsherds have had made-up inscrip- tions added to them.

In the eighteenth century Europe 'discovered' a taste for Chinese ceramics. Here a field opened up for the forger to exploit the incautious collector or museum curator. But the profession of faker knows no boundaries, for the Chinese themselves had already been at the task. Examples date well back into history, some objects either innocent imitations or fraudulently produced copies were made as long ago as the year one thousand. Pieces of pure Chinese porcelain, which was a development from stoneware, were first produced between A.D. 618 and 906 during the T'ang Dynasty. It was at this time that a number of the examples had the delightful white Hsingyae and celadon-green glazes that hold such an attraction for the connoisseur. Coupled with this the attention of the collectors was drawn to the exquisitely modelled horses, camels and other animals with the highest popularity for the figures of Chinese ladies. The at times grotesque and powerful tomb figures have also caught the fancy of many. This increasing market did not go unnoticed; for a Professor Yetts who visited some of the places that were working on T'ang copies, wrote: 'In 1912 I visited a factory at Peking where along shelves stood hundreds of newly-made figures. Comparison of these with the genuine originals which had served as patterns proved that certain modern replicas may defy detection.' Oriental pottery as a whole has a very hard glaze which is a considerable help to the forger as he does not have to go to all the trouble of falsifying the surface and giving the pieces other signs of age.

In the eighteenth century the Chinese collectors themselves had a great vogue for Sung ware. So much so that pieces from the Imperial collection of this period were sent to a factory at Ching-te-chen to be copied and then produced as legitimate imitations which were generally marked with the current reign periods as a guard against being passed off as genuine. Some astute craftsmen soon found that these date marks could fairly simply be ground off and a profitable sale made. As an example of a successful take-in of a top person, there is a piece of this copied ware in the British Museum forgery collection that apparently fooled the Emperor Ch'ien Lung, for on it he wrote a passage in praise of Sung Imperial ware.

The master potters and factories of Europe have not been neglected by the forger. One of the most distinctive artists in the ceramic field was Bernard Palissy. He had as great a popularity in his own lifetime as he has today with collectors. His method, which allowed for the building up of elaborate groups of animal, fish and plant life on his pieces, was his own

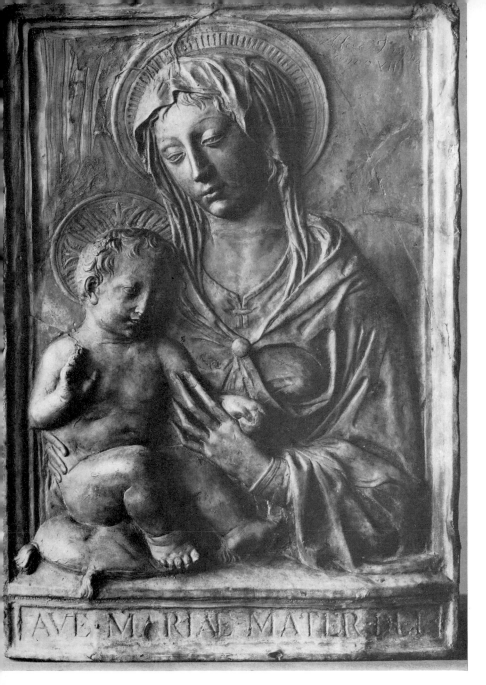

Plate 20. *Madonna and Child by Alceo Dossena.*
By courtesy of the Victoria and Albert Museum.

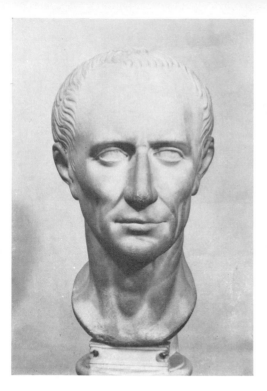

Plate 21. Portrait Bust of Julius Caesar—eighteenth century imitation after the antique. Courtesy of the Trustees of the British Museum.

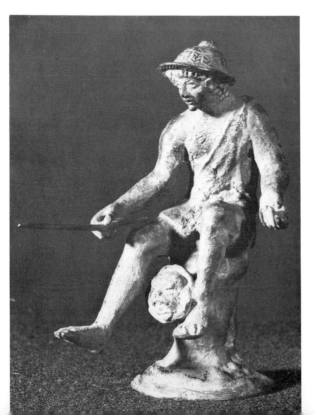

Plate 22. A bronze Greek statuette allegedly 600 B.C., which was proven as false after examination by an X-ray fluorescence spectrometer. By courtesy of the National Museum of Antiquities for Scotland and Nuclear Enterprises Limited.

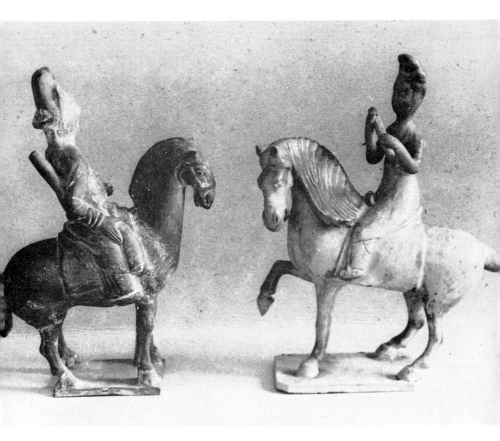

Plate 23. On the left a good copy of a Wei Dynasty Equestrian Figure, made in August 1923.
On the right a bad copy of an Equestrienne Lady Musician, made since 1945. Courtesy of Mr. Kiddell of Sotheby's.

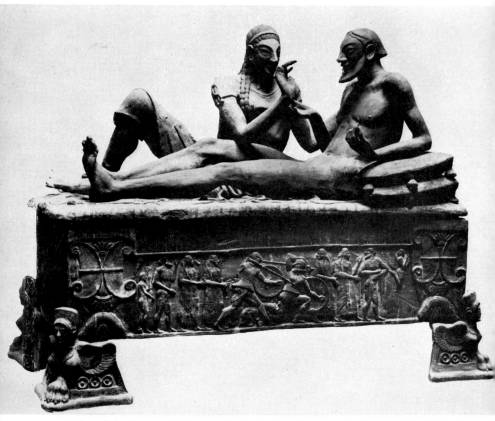

*Plate 24. Terra-cotta. So-called Tanagra style
purporting to be of the late IV and III centuries* B.C.
Courtesy of the Trustees of the British Museum.

discovery. Records show that even when he was living, and he was working for Catherine de' Medici, Queen of France, as early as 1570, copyists were at their game. A number of potters spent much time and energy trying to find out exactly what was his technique. One of the most successful some time later was Jean Charles Avisseau (1796–1861). His imitations of Palissy ware found a ready demand and have posed much trouble for the expert, particularly as there are no certain cases of authentification from Bernard Palissy.

The clear-cut easily recognizable work of Della Robbia has beckoned to the forger, and although the expert in this field is unlikely to be taken in, the not-so-well-read collector can fall for the deceptions. There have been of course numerous imitations taken from original Della Robbias and definitely sold as such. In the nineteenth century there was a Frenchman, Joseph Devers, who imitated more successfully than most the Italian faience, so much so that he was able to sell some of his work to the Sèvres Museum. Here again, though, these productions of the last century that took in the experts, if looked at today appear almost obviously false. But this is the same story as with many fakes; once they have been exposed the deception appears almost brash.

What has caused much confusion in the ceramic field was that, particularly in Europe, as fresh manufactories opened and produced popular wares other factories 'jumped on the band-wagon' and started to produce good copies of their opponents' shapes and designs. Unfortunately even the marks were purloined into the bargain. The position for the collector becomes decidedly awkward and much delving into provenance is needed to ensure authenticity.

The faker of ceramics working today has many devices. The network of cracks in the glaze can be produced in a somewhat similar way to the cracking in paint and varnish films. With ceramics this can be done by arranging that there will be a difference in the shrinkage of the clay and glaze when fired. If the clay shrinks less than the glaze, a crack network can be produced similar to that found on Chinese or Japanese vases. If the clay shrinks more than the glaze, the latter is liable to flake and peel off. If the forger practises with this formula he can produce characteristic imperfections that are sometimes found with antique ware. Further age impersonation can be imparted by holding the object over a bundle of lit tapers that will emit heavy black smoke. The oily smoke marks can then be rubbed into the cracks; this will help to remove the new look of a freshly carried out technique. Too perfect a glaze can be treated with hydrofluoric acid to produce convincing imperfections. Where a forger has built up a pastiche he may have had to actually fabricate pieces to complete the build-up. The most expert method here is for the fragment to be moulded to a shape in clay and then fired. For the unskilled hand this is fraught with difficulty as it is not at all easy to judge the shrinkage that will take place during firing. The more common way is to make up a paste of a plaster with a glue which can then be modelled to the required shape, and when nearly hard be pared with a scalpel and then sanded smooth. Much of the touching in of colours for the decoration has been done with oil colours. When these have hardened a resin varnish can be applied.

A suspect object can be examined with an ultra-violet light in a dark room; this in many cases will expose the work by the appearance of fluorescence. A secondary method to detect a recent forgery of this type can be to gently warm the object. This will generally affect the fresh varnish and oil paint so that it will become tacky and also give off a slight resin and oily smell.

Marks on the various wares should always be very carefully checked. Not only will the faker fiddle them but also he is sometimes careless and does not study the history of the particular factory he is aping. Thus he will put on a mark which may be correct in principle for the maker but will be out of datal order for the production of the type copied.

Glass probably offers the forger less scope than with other categories. The very nature of the material is less pliant to treatment and the use of artifices. Such naive forgeries of Roman glass that have been made with iridescence simulated by fish scales stuck on the inside would fool few today.

Other attempts to give glass the visual effect of age have been made by burial in moist earth in an effort to bring on the cloudiness associated with objects of some periods. Pristine surfaces can also be brought down by carefully swabbing over with hydrofluoric acid. Iridescence can be induced by the choice course of leaving the fake immured in a well matured heap of stable dung. The problem for the forger with all these devices is that they will produce an iridescence or 'ageing' layer that is all in one piece, whereas as mentioned in Chapter Six the scientists have found that it is a gradual building up of layers and thus examination by an expert can soon expose the fraud.

Attempts may be made to colour modern glass so as to simulate the products of specific periods. The surface inside the vessel can first be slightly roughened by acid and then some form of dye applied. When this is dry a hard-drying clear varnish can be put on to bring back the surface. A solvent which will not attack glass such as acetone will quickly lay bare this treatment. Wheel and diamond engraving by a recent hand will generally show up when compared to genuine work of the period; the faked decoration will often appear weak and have a powdery look. Some lesser hands try to pass off crude put-togethers. Here they will have joined odd stems and bowls, perhaps even using a grinder to alter shapes or remove chips and defects. The trained eye will normally be able to sense something is adrift. Comparison with the true will show up faults in style.

Fraud with silver objects to a degree falls into a category of its own. For here most of the deception is carried out not so much as straightforward forgery but rather by fiddling with objects that have already been made by genuine craftsmen. This practice is encouraged largely by the fact that in many cases the would-be collector reaches for his magnifying glass to read the mark before he uses his aesthetic and stylistic sense.

The all important hall-marking was brought in as long ago as 1300, when on 26 September of that year it was made a law by a statute. The system if honoured carries with it a guarantee of purity for the gold or silver and a protection from fakes for the collector. Since the introduction of hall-marking the control has lain with the Worshipful Company of Goldsmiths. Sadly the 'wide' boys can lay traps for the unwary and at times the expert by falsifying the hall-marks. This can be done in a number of ways. Casts can be taken from genuine pieces of silver. There is a snag here for the faker; his cast should only be used on a single piece; for if he intends to make a set of goblets or dishes it will soon become apparent that there is something odd about the marking. There will be a regularity in the spacing which would not occur with such exactitude if the pieces were genuine and were being individually marked at the assay office. The forger can make himself a set of punches bearing the requisite marks. These have been made from brass and steel; the use of the latter being more difficult to detect as they will tend to give better impressions. The cleverest method as far as the forger is concerned is to cut out the hall-marks from an old piece of plate and insert them into another article. This was a fairly common practice during the first half of the eighteenth century, and the pieces most popular to try it on were sauce-boats, bowls, cups and casters. Probably at that time one of the main reasons was not to deceive but to avoid paying the threepence or so per ounce duty on silver that was then levied. Modern practitioners of this artifice would be more intent on either giving the object a greater antiquity or using the device to pass off sub-standard silver in the main body of the object.

Alteration of use of an object is against the law. For example, a tankard once passed and hall-marked cannot then be made into a jug. Nor can base metal or more silver be added to an article, although later decoration in the way of engraving or chasing can be added. The re-working of plates has caught out many an unwary novice collector. This was a popular task in the latter part of the eighteenth century and is still being done. Generally they will be made up into shallow bowls, a gadrooned edge may be added and other channelled or repoussé decoration. If the hall-mark was reasonably near the edge of the original there is a chance that this practice will be shown up as the modelling and beating of the bowl shape can tend to cause distortion in the marks.

Despite unpleasant penalties likely to come their way, such as being pilloried and having an ear cut off, records show that the fiddlers were at it certainly as far back as the days of Queen Elizabeth I. Since that time there has been a series of laws intended to outlaw the various pranks which the tricksters have sought to get up to. The acting body has always been the Goldsmiths Company. Specimen prosecutions in the eighteenth century include: in 1767 the soldering of bits of sub-standard silver to shoe-buckles and tea-tongs and then sending them for assay in order to fraudulently obtain the requisite marks and in 1770 for selling silver watch-cases that had not been hall-marked. In 1773 it can be noted that the counterfeiting of hall-marks could bring the death penalty. An act of 1739 laid down that all silver wares should contain at least 11 ozs 2 dwts of fine silver in every pound weight Troy and that gold objects should not be less than 22 carats of fine gold.

An Act of 1844 set out clearly to define a string of offences which laid the perpetrator open to severe punishment. Section 2 of this Act gave the following:

Forging or counterfeiting any Die for marking Gold or Silver Wares or knowingly uttering the same;
Marking Wares with forged Dies, or uttering them;
Forging any Mark of any Die, or uttering the same;
Transposing or removing Marks, or uttering them;
Having in possession knowingly any such Die, or Ware marked with the same;
Cutting or severing Marks with Intent to affix them upon other Wares;
Affixing any Mark cut or severed from any other Wares;
Fraudulently using genuine Dies.

Section 3.

Selling or having possession of any Wares with forged or

transposed Marks without lawful excuse (even unknowingly that the Marks were so forged or transposed); penalty £10 each offence.

Section 4.

Dealers to be exempt from the above penalties on giving up the names of the actual manufacturer of such wares of gold or silver or base metal, or of the person from whom they received them, but not from the consequence of uttering them with guilty knowledge.

Section 9.

Dealers not to fraudulently erase, obliterate, or deface any mark under a penalty of £5.

In 1849 at Taunton there occurred an interesting legal wrangle which centred on the usage and meaning of the words transposition and addition. Two silversmiths were arraigned before the Assizes for having in their possession a silver spoon and soup-ladle which had on them marks transferred from silver skewers. The spoon and ladle were of modern manufacture but both bore the mark for the year 1744. An expert from the Goldsmiths' Company demonstrated that the objects had not been made in one piece but that the parts with the hall-marks had been inserted. The defence for the culprits centred on the weak plea that what they had done was addition rather than transposition. The purpose of the plea was to avoid the much stiffer penalty for the latter crime which was classed as a felony. The jury must have been impressed by the subtleties of argument as they let the wily characters off despite protests from the judge. A verdict here that they would be highly unlikely to get away with today.

The forger working now and setting out to make objects pertaining to date from the prime period of the eighteenth century or earlier and by master craftsmen of those times probably finds his hardest task is to simulate the weathering of his metal. Countless cleanings, often with too harsh a powder by rough handed footmen, and the general wear and tear of usage at table leave a tricky surface skin to emulate. Decoration becomes slightly blunted and often hard accretions of grime and remainders of polish build up in crevices. But more than that, the look of true old silver has some strange indefinable quality that cannot be aptly described other than to state it is something that one grows to understand and recognize. The forger may of course deliberately use abrasion on the hall-marks so that they become highly difficult to decipher and this particularly applies to the date shields. Practice in handling old and modern silver is the main protection. With objects such as bowls and others that have been put together by soldering there can be a conspicuous tonal and textural variance between the old and the new. Attempts may be made to blur the judgement by dulling the silver to give it a surface impression of age. Here the faker can deliberately apply a chemical that will speedily tarnish the metal. Recipes for this are various; including so called 'liver of sulphur', chloride of lime, and other agents which will encourage the formation of the dark brown-grey silver sulphide on the surface of the object. Actually today if the forger is working in an urban or industrial area the atmosphere will oblige by producing the tarnish for him fairly quickly. The polluted air can hold at times an alarming amount of sulphur in the form of sulphuretted hydrogen which comes from manufacturing fumes from factories. After darkening, the piece can be given a half-polish; this leaves a degree of tarnish in the crevices and modelling, and just brings up enough of the silver look to suggest a 'genuine' age and to whet the appetite.

Objects making somewhat weak claims to be antique silver may be come across in German silver, Britannia plate, and can carry hall-marks; but as their deceptive powers are poor a good class forger would disdain such practice.

Relics of man's warlike past have always had a fascination for collectors. Body armour and weapons seem to hold an intriguing power for some. Recently a workshop in Spain has been seeing to it that supplies are kept up. A suit of armour in the hall, a bascinet hanging on the wall can produce an aura that must hark back to the days of glamour and chivalry and provide some sense of accomplishment now only felt in dreams. In the nineteenth century armour fakers were at work to people the dark halls of Victorian success with ghostly figures that gathered dust and rust. The steel was subjected to all manners of maltreatment. It was roasted with fire, steeped in acid and buried; anything to give it the well pitted rusted look that would make the unwary fall for its age. The savaged surfaces would then be burnished up. With many of the fakers the craftsmanship was poor and they often did not pay enough attention to design and decoration. Features were freely adapted from seals and miniatures in medieval manuscripts and further embellished by purely imaginative representations. In many cases little enough care was taken to relate the pieces to the body that was supposed to go inside them. There have been helmets made which if worn and the visor had been closed would have sliced off the nose. Gauntlets were produced with the thumb-pieces halfway up the wrists. The plates with which the pieces were constructed gave the appearance of having been rolled from old sheets of iron or chimney pipes being riveted together with nothing more than round-headed nails; the edges of the plates themselves giving the look of having been cut clumsily with metal shears. Yet in their time objects such as these found their way through the guard of many collectors, caused much argument amongst antiquarians, and even for a short time held honoured display positions in the Tower of London, until they were exposed and returned to the anonymity they deserved.

One of the most famous pieces that turned up was the so-called 'Faversham' helm, an English forgery of the mid-nineteenth century aping the style of the mid–twelfth century. At the time there was much irate argument centred around this imitation of a nasal-bar helm. It was said to have been found in Faversham church, and there associations were claimed for it with the lives of King Stephen and his son Eustace. When no buyer was found in this country it was sold abroad and for a time was exhibited in the Musée d'Artillerie, Paris.

In this century the skills of the forger in this field have increased although there still appear serious faults with the imitating of the designs from different periods. 'Maximilian' suits of armour were forged with at times the eye-slits set at far too an oblique angle for the wearer to see properly. The fluting lacked

subtleties of the real thing. With the genuine articles the channel-
ling had a section of concave grooves between each ridge, whilst
with the false this section was simply left flat. Moreover the
mechanical performance of the fakes lacked much in elegance.
This is noticeable most with the legs which are at times clumsy
whilst the originals were slender and gracefully shaped.

Much of the fake armour and weapons has originated in
Germany and Italy. Nuremberg and Lucca have both given
cover to skilled craftsmen. From the former came highly finished
and ornamented suits and from the latter convincing imitations
of old daggers.

Out and out faking with clocks is a comparative rarity. With
these it is much more a case of marriage or perhaps this could be
better expressed as polygamy. As specimens in the past and today
have become more and more decrepit, restorer-clockmakers have
accumulated a store of cases, faces, works and the rest. All too
often is come across an example which on close examination
yields a wide and diverse pedigree. The field of clocks of
whatever type is one of the most specialized and calls for the
dedicated expert to be able to find the way through the com-
plexities to the entirely genuine.

To a degree the whole field of collecting can be divided into
two; the majority seeking for the fine, beautiful and rare, with a
select number making for the objects that are connected with a
particular use, items that in themselves may not necessarily have
aesthetic quality or be made from valued materials. Into this
latter category come scientific instruments which appeal to a
comparatively small number of collectors. Navigational aids,
telescopes, sundials, orreries and past laboratory equipment do
not really attract the forger. Mainly because the amount of
exacting work involved is not commensurate with the limited
return he can expect from the small possible market. A few
examples of Middle Eastern origin have drifted across the scene,
but these often have fairly obvious defects either in design or
inscription, or are of degraded workmanship.

Another field in which the forger seldom preys is that of
textiles. Here again he knows that the returns are likely to be
meagre and he also realizes that the technical demands are stiff

and time for execution can be lengthy. There are however devices that can be used to transform the surface appearance of textiles which may catch the unwary.

Middle Eastern and Oriental rugs are now very much rising in popularity as collectors' items and offer themselves as a possible for the faker. To a degree the geometric simplicity of some patterns lends itself to copying. Although it is unlikely that the forger will be able to compete with the very fine knotting of the finest specimens; a careful look at the back of the rug should always be taken to note the concentration. Study should be made of the pattern motifs because the forger is not always as careful as he should be and there can be divergences in the use of a particular design out of context historically. It is quite possible for him also to alter colours. Generally with this fraud he will pick on a cheap and lower quality rug and attempt by the use of dyes to give it a false appearance. Synthetic surface treatments can further seemingly impart a feeling of softness. Modern artificial threads can be treated to give the look and feel of silk. If he tries to simulate a genuine old rug by mechanical weaving he is in trouble. The machine will always produce a high degree of regularity which when compared to a true original will show up. A hand-worked example, however skilled, will exhibit slight irregularities in the knotting. The fringe on a rug can also be a guide. With a machine made copy this will be worked as a separate piece that is fixed later whilst the real fringe is produced from the knotting of the threads used in the weaving.

Antique velvets and other precious fabrics have been attempted by the forger using modern weaving methods. Although the Jacquard method will make very passable representations of almost any pattern programmed into it, there is never quite the right feel of the resulting example. After weaving, the operator can then attempt to age his product. He must try to bring on the essential harmony of colours that is so much in evidence with the masters' fabrics from the past. The piece can be left outside to the mercy of sunshine and rain. Steam jets may be applied or he may resort to a device similar to an overall glaze for a painting. A bath of slightly toned dye can be prepared and the whole piece of fabric lowered into it. This can, if carefully done, be misleading as the end result will seem to have a gentle appearance of aged harmony.

Faked examples of embroidery can normally be picked up by the close examination of the threads used. Machine spun yarns have a very different look from the product of hand spinning. Artificial gold and silver threads bear only a passing resemblance to the real thing. Tapestries as entire examples are unlikely to be tackled by the forger. But severely damaged ones from the past will in many cases have had considerable areas re-worked. It is obviously desirable that the extent of such restoration should be known. The repairs may have been carried out by a trained expert using every effort with materials and technique. They may on the other hand have been made using threads that come close to deception. With these the threads used can have been of a low neutral colour and then coloured afterwards rather in the manner of retouching a painting. Examples have appeared where the threads have been brushed with egg tempera which will leave a matt finish that will not stand out from the genuine old threads or even at times the simulator has been known to use pastel. A gentle folding of the suspected area should expose this artifice as the underlying colour of the threads can be seen.

Lastly in the field of adornment comes jewellery, and here for centuries, copies and outright deceptions have appeared. These may range from the highly sophisticated work of craftsmen such as Ruchomovsky with his Saitaphernes tiara (mentioned in Chapter Three) down to the mass produced examples of scarabs that are set in often quite atrocious settings that have neither an appearance of age nor even an attempt at quality in design or workmanship. During the eighteenth century there was a considerable fashion for antique jewellery which provided a prosperous market for the faker. Undoubtedly a number of these fraudulent pieces are still winging their way through the channels of exchange. Cameo portraits were in demand; some carried out with great skill by hands that were adept at aping the manners of their betters. Here various ageing devices could be employed to remove the 'brightness' of a newly made piece; one such was to immerse for short periods in weak acid or lye. Genuine gems could have their pristine cuts purposely chipped; they could be shaken in containers of harsh sand to impart a slight scratching.

The scientist with cold, calculated clinical methods today can expose the forgery which will appear in any field, it is hoped, but he must be led to it. Yet still that vital first defence is the sheer experience and knowledge of the trained eye. The sense developed with time by the connoisseur that enables him to feel a sympathy, a bond with the true creative genius whose mind and hand brought into being the masterpiece or humble object. The real has an indefinable breath of truth that escapes the false. This gentle zephyr must be cultivated and followed until an awakened aesthetic mind will be alert to warning signals.

5 *The Scribe*

MANUSCRIPT AND BOOK COLLECTORS GENERALLY FALL into one of two categories; those who are interested in the texts and editions, and those who prize more the bindings of the volumes. It might be supposed that here could be a field which would not have a great attraction for the forger, but alas, no; for these gentlemen go on the theory if someone wants it they will very soon produce it if the legitimate source gives signs of drying-up. The act of forging may have in some cases a psychological impetus as with Chatterton, who was mentioned in Chapter One; it may be triggered off for reasons of self-justification; but more generally it is for the good old-fashioned gain motive. The last was obviously the spur in the eighteenth century in France. Fashion dictated that rare editions were the 'in thing'. Some characters then saw that it would be worth all the trouble and cost to produce the supply for the market. In Lyons there were craftsmen printers at work on Racine's writings. In Rouen a spate of Molière's work appeared. Here the specialists went to great trouble to reproduce not only the type but also decorative details and the paper. The expense in outlay was probably soon met as it is on record that a first edition of Molière's writings, which was dated 1669, fetched a price of 15,000 francs in Paris. Thomas Wise the book forger (mentioned in Chapter Two) would have done well to follow the care, particularly with his papers, of the French gentlemen working about two hundred years earlier.

Modern photo-mechanical printing processes can very well copy not only type but also illustrations. More than that, specialist paper-mills can provide fair imitations of papers if given a sample. Experts are unlikely to be fooled; a judicious use of a magnifying glass will likely as not show surface differences in the paper; some claim that a high powered magnification will show variations in the ink edges of the type as it presses into the paper. But these fakes are not aimed at the erudite. Their market is in a much wider field where the knowledge is less but the money is more. Today there are being produced an increasingly large number of fascimile editions of fine volumes from the past. The excellence of some of these could be an enticement to the fraudulent minded; for a little fiddling, a modicum of rebinding could possibly turn these innocently made books into passable currency.

Bookbindings have in many ways attracted more attention from the forger than the printed matter inside. The simplest way for the crooked minded was hardly to indulge in faking at all, just a straightforward matter of transfer. Exquisite bindings could be taken from one book and put on another to raise the price of the latter. More advanced trickery could be to use old leathers already decorated, or to add to the decoration. Fragments from several pieces of truly antique leather could be built up into a binding in the manner of a pastiche with painting.

In the period between the seventeenth and nineteenth centuries there were several active centres reaping a good living from this type of chicanery. One of the most skilled men behind the scenes was a Monsieur Hagué who worked during the latter part of the 1800s in Brussels, London and Paris. Vittorio Villa centred his productions in Bologna and Milan. A pet ploy was to procure old and original iron stamps that had been used for impressing the blind-tooling or gold leaf decoration on to covers. Armed with these the forger could fabricate bindings complete or often an easier way would be to add material to an already bound book; the idea being to make the victim think that he was buying a volume that had once had its place in some great collection. Monograms, coats of arms and emblems are amongst the additions that have been made. Experience and knowledge are in the armour needed to protect against such falsifications.

The forger often may have ruined his handiwork by spoiling the overall design of the original; details may have been added that crowd or encroach on the design or include quite stupid anachronisms.

A fine volume, unless it has a complete and faultless provenance, should be examined with care to note if there are details that point to the activities of the faker. If there are doubts, an experienced scholar and bookbinder should be consulted. Qualified restoration is one matter but fraudulent reconstruction is another. How a book is put together can often give away an otherwise skilled fake. Examine carefully the gilded ornament. That which is a genuine example from the past very often has a refinement about it; the stamping appears more clear cut, as against the tooling of today which tends to have a heavier feel in the actual impression. The use of a strong glass can bring up imperfections in the application of the gold leaf, there can be signs of fraying and small gaps. This is partly due to the lack of skill in the forger and to a degree to the fact that the gold leaf of today tends to be somewhat thinner and is also at times not so evenly beaten out in manufacture.

If it is suspected that the binding has been faked from new leather, close examination should be able to show this up. However well a leather bound book, say from the seventeenth century, had been looked after, it would be unlikely to have no scars. Look well at the hinges of the binding where it would most certainly have some sign of wear. As the book would have been opened again and again, this part of the leather would have been frequently tensioned and a pulling or fraying of the fibres would have occurred. Observe the bottom edges of the binding where the book would have been exposed to friction as it was pulled out of the shelf and replaced. The forger can attempt to simulate this mark of age, but leather is not the easiest material to manipulate in this way. Patination of leather needs time and simulated finishes tend to have gloss rather than the soft sheen and the feel the genuine acquires with years of handling.

Incomplete rare volumes can have their needs attended to by the talents of an expert with pen and ink. Frontispieces and missing pages have been most convincingly faked in this manner.

Illuminated manuscripts in general have escaped the attention of the forger, partially because of the technical details involved and perhaps more so from the fact that until the nineteenth century they were sought after by comparatively few collectors. In the early centuries they suffered more from alteration and the addition of spurious details; these being brought about often as not from a desire to challenge a thesis or to refute the claim of an originator than with a desire for monetary gain.

Many libraries have collections of literary fakes. These are really in a separate class from the foregoing as their perpetrators are in many cases doing a Van Meegeren in print. They are concerned with the making up of the actual text; this may be to imitate the work of a known writer, to falsify some aspect of history, or, as in the case of Vrain Lucas, for what amounts to a quick and easy 'con' of a scholar who should have known a great deal better. The victim in this well publicized case of the nineteenth century in Paris was one Monsieur Chasles a member of a famous French Académie des Sciences and a celebrated mathematician. He had one particular weakness, he liked to collect letters and autographs and this is a decidedly tricky field in which to ferret out the true and the false. Seldom has a learned mind been taken for such a ride. Vrain Lucas, in all, took him for some 140,000 francs worth for a collection of sheer rubbish. The gorgeous selection included a letter from Mary Magdalen to Lazarus, also from Cleopatra to Caesar, a passport signed by Vercingetorix, and other letters purporting to have been written by Pontius Pilate, Alexander the Great, Attila, Joan of Arc, Cervantes, Shakespeare, Dante and Luther. More extraordinary still, these were all written in French, except one from Galileo, which was in Italian, and were in an idiom that was suited to the eighteenth century. There were some 27,000 items in all. Vrain Lucas told his prey that they had come from the collection made by the Compte de Boisjardin who had conveniently emigrated to America in 1791 but sadly on the way he had been ship-wrecked and drowned. In some miraculous manner the letters had been saved, all practically undamaged except for a few that had received a soaking.

Nothing can quite compete with the foregoing but there have

Plate 25. A sugar bowl and cover c. 1720. A 'Duty Dodger'. By courtesy of John Shearlock, Esq.

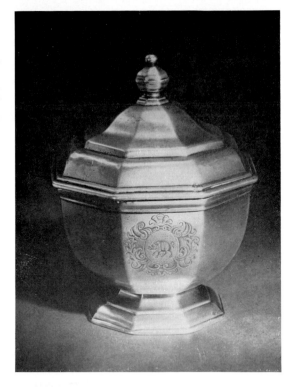

Plate 26. When the foot was detached it showed how a disc of silver had been inserted bearing the hallmark from another item. By courtesy of John Shearlock, Esq.

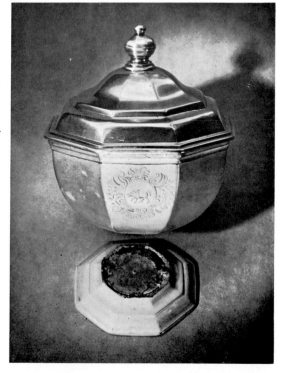

*Plate 27. A fine copy of
an Irish Decanter,
moulded on the base
'Cork Glass Company',
c. 1925. The glass is too
heavy; the milling of
the collars too regular.
The original would be
1810. Courtesy of Mr.
Kiddell of Sotheby's.*

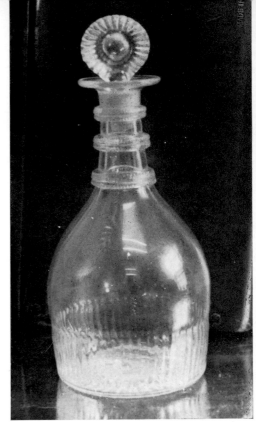

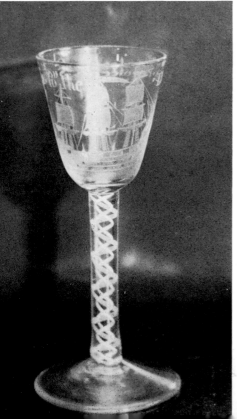

*Plate 28. A Privateer
Wine Glass superbly
engraved with the
privateer and inscribed
'Success to the Lyon
Privateer'. (Actually by
1759 the vessel had
become a slaver.) This
glass was made in the
twentieth century.
Courtesy of Mr. Kiddell
of Sotheby's.*

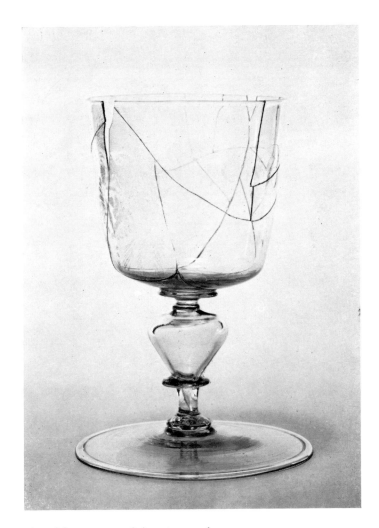

Plate 29. Forgery of the nineteenth century, pretending to be seventeenth century. Known as the Barnvellt Glass. Courtesy of the Trustees of the British Museum.

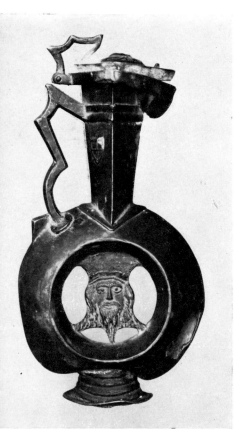

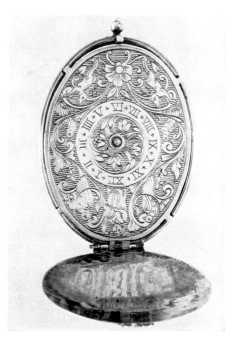

Plate 30. Billy and Charley in a more ambitious mood; a strange ewer from their hands. Courtesy of the Trustees of the British Museum.

Plate 31. Nineteenth-century forgery of a watch, professing to be seventeenth century. Courtesy of the Trustees of the British Museum.

been many others who have reached for the chair of greatness via the pen. In the ninth century a stir must have been caused by the arrival on the literary scene of a set of Decretals. This contained amongst other material, documents supporting the Papal claim to temporal power, about a hundred letters from the early popes, and also included was the famous 'Donation of Constantine'. The author took the name of Isidore, archbishop of Seville who died in 636. The forgery lasted well for it was not until the fifteenth century that it was exposed by Laurentius Valla, the great Humanist.

England in the eighteenth century produced a batch of over-imaginative fellows. There was James Macpherson, who under the name of Ossian, a kind of northern Homer, produced Gaelic epics. He even had the gall to stand up to Samuel Johnson to try to prove the stories were not fakes. Shakespeare has often drawn the attentions of the faker. In 1794/5 appeared deeds and signatures pertaining to be of or relating to the great poet. These were the work of William Henry Ireland (1777–1835), son of Samuel Ireland the engraver. He had access to Elizabethan parchments in the lawyer's office where he worked. He went further and made up two pseudo-Shakespearian plays: 'Vortigern and Rowena' and 'Henry II', which fooled many of the then experts and men of scholarship. Sheridan produced the former of these at Drury Lane in 1796, but it was a flop. Ireland did eventually have the good grace to admit to his fraud.

How much more of this game can still lie hidden in private libraries and collections can only be surmised.

6 *Anti-forgery Weapons*

FOR THE ULTIMATE DECISION, SCIENCE CAN RALLY A formidable investigation outfit with detecting instruments and techniques for the examination of a suspect, which the forger of today knows he must attempt to defeat. To a degree he takes the gamble that he will be able to launch his products in such a way as to make his money through the ignorance of those customers who first come into contact with his progeny, or he may be able to dupe and mesmerize others with high-sounding provenance. What he dreads is that he will come under the scrutiny of a trained eye which will start off a chain reaction of thorough laboratory testing. Today there are so many hurdles to clear that it is unlikely he will be able to deceive the clinical step-by-step investigation the scientists can initiate.

A preliminary examination of a doubtful painting apparently from the sixteenth century could be by the application of a solvent such as toluene to a small area near the edge. Oil paint once thoroughly dry can be very resistant and no colour should come away. Therefore if such a test was made on a work, for example, thought to be by an early artist such as Cranach, and the paint softened and came away doubts would be raised as to its truth. But this is a method that should only be carried out by a trained hand. With some early artists such as Rembrandt there could be a reaction and considerable damage done. It should be emphasized that any solvent and chemical treatments of works of art in any category are strictly the province of the laboratory where protective steps will be known and adhered to.

Two branches of black and white photography can be helpful in the early stages of an examination. These are photomicrography and macrophotography. The former simply means the taking of a photograph through a microscope. Adapters for many cameras, especially the small 35 mm models, can be obtained which makes it possible to fix them to the eyepieces of microscopes. This method allows for a high magnification in taking the initial negative which can be increased still further by enlargement. Large blow-ups of details in brushwork and decoration when compared to similar enlargement with known authentic examples can often point to the lie straight away.

Macrophotography is a method whereby the camera is fitted with a 'macro lens', special extension tubes or bellows which will enable it to produce a life-size image of the object or area being taken on the negative. This will allow for very high definition on a print. Macrophotography is useful for the examination of details such as signatures on paintings or drawings, for recording stamps or taking a searching look at small objects such as jewellery, coins and medals.

Photography used as above adds a greater strength to the eye, but when it is coupled with X-rays, ultraviolet rays or infrared light, it brings into being a visual detective that can see where the eye cannot.

X-rays must be amongst the weapons particularly feared by the forger, as they have the power of penetrating most materials and therefore of clearly showing underlying work. This may be layers of paint and details of the support, or construction and fixing with furniture. An X-ray of a fake Sienese triptych (supposedly fifteenth century) by Ioni, who was active before the last war, showed up amongst other things how the forger had used modern nails in constructing parts of the panels. X-rays when used on the Van Meegeren 'Vermeers' clearly showed up how he had used canvases which had already been painted on, as residual images of the earlier pictures showed through. One forger rather foolishly tried to protect his fake by covering the canvas before starting to paint with a thin sheet of lead. This device was immediately laid bare when subjected to X-rays.

Museum laboratories can employ X-ray photography for the non-destructive examination of suspected antiquities. The technique will show up concealed inlays and decoration and give clues as to the way the objects were made. The principle is that as X-rays pass through the specimen the materials of which it is made will absorb more or less of the rays. By learning to 'read' the tonal densities the operator can learn much which by normal observation would be invisible.

One of the most readily available and simplest methods of picking up additions, alterations or restorations to works of art is the use of ultraviolet radiation. The rays can be artificially produced by employing a mercury vapour lamp. The radiation is a band that is just beyond the visible range on the violet end of the spectrum. The examination or photography by ultraviolet radiation should take place in a darkened room. Many substances when exposed to a beam from an ultraviolet-ray producing lamp, which has had visible light removed by a special filter, will fluoresce in colours and a manner that are characteristic of particular materials. The photography using ultraviolet rays can be done in two ways; the fluorescent-light method and the reflected-light. With the first a filter is placed over the lens of the camera that will absorb the reflected ultraviolet rays but at the same time allow a photograph to be taken of the visible fluorescence. If, for example, a painting was being examined that was suspected of being altered by a later hand, and there was a time gap of upwards of fifty years between the original and alteration or addition, in general this would show up by a glow. Alterations to the surface of ceramics which are invisible to the naked eye will be clearly shown up. Changes and restorations on most objects will reveal themselves. The reflected-light method is made by ultraviolet light thrown back from whatever is being examined. The filter being used this time on the lens of the camera lets the ultraviolet radiation through to the film but stops visible radiation.

Examination by ultraviolet radiation would uncover a recently forged marble statue claiming to be of considerable age. There would be a difference in fluorescence between a genuine example and the fake which would be caused by the genuine patination of the authentic work that would have had its surface layers worked on by natural weathering; whereas such a condition would not be present in the newly worked forgery, however astute the 'bent' craftsman had been with applied ageing devices. The reaction of woods depends to a degree on their surface finishes.

Infra-red rays are nonactinic and can be detected by their thermal effect. As their name suggests they are a range of radiation which lies just beyond the red end of the visible spectrum. One of their greatest uses is that the rays will go through even dark and obscured areas. This characteristic can often mean that inscriptions and writing, particularly with old manuscripts, can be deciphered and separated. There have been examples of illegible writing on blackened leather scrolls which were revealed by infra-red. The reason for this is that the leather would still reflect the infra-red light but the carbon in the ink would not. In a case like this the infra-red photograph would show a white background against which the ink characters would stand out quite clearly.

An infra-red photograph of an oil painting could easily show up much of the underpainting and initial drawing. These factors can be compared with known mannerisms of the artist in other works.

In the taking of photographs, whether black and white or colour, of works of art the best aesthetic light arrangement may not necessarily be that which will tell most about the object being assessed. If a raking light, that is, one which is placed at an acute angle to one side or the other, or above or below, again at a low angle, is used it can at times bring out qualities that just cannot be noted with conventional lighting. For the best results the light source should have some kind of directional shade that will be able to play a beam on to the surface being examined. This form of lighting will make clearly visible areas of impasto and slight deficiencies in surfaces that have been altered; even quite shallow indentations will be clear.

Chemical analysis is another potent and generally unanswerable agent in the war against the wiles of the forger. There have been a number of cases where these gentlemen, particularly if operating in the field of antiquities, have gone to considerable trouble to bury their products in an area where they might be expected to be found and if possible where an excavation was either going on or was shortly to begin. Such an object could be a small statuette pertaining to be Roman and seemingly to be bronze. The site of excavation might be in the area of an early Roman town or encampment. Analysis could quickly show that the figure was not bronze but zinc. If in this case the metal was pure it could be convincing evidence that the statuette was a fake because the Romans did not have pure zinc. If there were traces of other metals present they could be pointers to the origin of the piece.

With metal objects a knowledge of where ores with certain impurities are found can be invaluable when investigating some specimens. Here, though, the chemist may have to combine intuition with exact information, for some older ore deposits may have been worked out and their location lost to us. Further, scrap metal from many different areas may have been melted together and used by the original craftsmen to make some objects, and this same method can quite easily be aped by the forger.

When someone goes in for faking antiquities and hopes to get away with it he should have very considerable knowledge of the techniques of the ancients or he can quite easily be caught out by the laboratory. Small bronze figures such as that mentioned above are favourite targets; but crude attempts such as the pure zinc example are quickly exposed.

There is little doubt that bronze was first employed in Asia. Its entry in to Europe was likely via Ur where there is evidence of its use from about 3500 B.C. The history of the discovery of bronze and the working methods with the alloy are long and complicated with many pitfalls for the unwary.

The forger can be in difficulties in the composition of the alloy. Bronze today generally has between 9 or 10 per cent of tin. But with the ancient bronzes this proportion to copper could vary from about 2 per cent to 16 per cent. The early Egyptians at times added lead to their bronze probably to facilitate casting. They are also known to have combined copper lead alloys and bronze. A situla was found with a bronze core and a coating of copper lead alloy, which could have been done to simulate silver.

The early Egyptian bronzes on analysis show considerable variation in the proportions of copper and tin. This may have been because the various metalsmiths wanted to have more control over the working qualities of the alloy.

In contrast, when the chemist comes to the bronze of the early Greeks and Romans he finds that there appears to be less divergence with the recipes used, although there is an appreciable difference with the alloys of these two civilizations. The early Greek bronze had a fairly high proportion of tin with a negligible amount of lead, whilst the Roman bronze was low on tin and high on lead.

When the forger has solved the problem about the make-up of the bronze he is still faced with the techniques of working the alloy. Small figures were generally cast solid with larger ones being cast hollow. In Egypt the limbs of the larger figures were often cast separately and then attached to the bodies afterwards by mortise and tenon joints that had been shaped before the casting. The smaller figures, which would be solid, were cast by the *cire perdue* (lost wax) process. With this a model in beeswax would be made either by hand or moulded and then covered with malleable clay. The whole would then be heated, the wax would run away through a hole and the mould would become hard. Molten bronze was then poured in and when everything was cool the hardened clay would be broken away and finishing touches to the figure given with chisels. Hollow objects were cast in a near similar manner. With the larger figures or pieces the choice of hollow casting can have had three reasons. There was a saving in the amount of bronze and beeswax, also there would be a very appreciable cutting down in weight of the finished piece. When working, first of all a core for the object would be made to the rough shape required but smaller. This core could be of quartz sand which had been mixed with some organic material to provide modelling qualities. Next the core would be covered with a layer of beeswax, and into this the surface details would be worked. After that the procedure was the same as for solid casting. The whole would be covered with clay to form the outside mould, and heat applied to remove the wax and then, when hard and cool, the molten bronze would be poured in.

Examples of forged ancient glass are comparatively rare; for, again, the faker needs highly specialized knowledge if he can hope to evade detection. Museum laboratories have carried out very extensive work in this field and the results are readily obtainable for comparison. Objects from many places and times have been analysed including early Egypt, the Roman Empire, the Near and Far East, Russia and Medieval and Renaissance times in Europe. The outcome of this work has brought to light the conclusion that craftsmen in different places and at varying periods added constituents to their glasses that would not only affect the working properties of the glass but also the colour and transparency.

Microanalysis of more than two hundred objects of clear glass selected from the Middle East, Europe and North Africa and dating between the fifteenth century B.C. and twelfth century A.D. has been carried out. This has disclosed that there are fairly definite divisions in the constituents used to make the glass. Between the sixth century B.C. and the fourth century A.D. the glass had a fairly high content of antimony. From the fourth until the ninth century it was high in manganese but low in antimony. The early Islamic glasses from the eighth to the tenth century had neither antimony nor manganese but were high in magnesium and potassium.

Having achieved his correct chemistry for making up the glass, the problem is by no means over for the forger; for he is still left with probably the most difficult part in the manufacture of his 'pretender'. He has to make it look old. Weathering is almost always present with ancient glasses which have been exposed to one or other corrosive conditions. It generally appears as iridescence or a very thin cloudy crust. This crust is normally only a fraction of a millimetre thick but examples have come to light where the crust has been up to 4 mm thick. The snag for the forger with these weathering crusts is that almost invariably they have a layered structure which has a relationship to dendrochronology, in that a count of the weathered layers can give an approximate dating. The glasses that are most readily datable by this manner are those through the medieval period up to the early eighteenth century. Roman and Byzantine glasses are normally too corrosion resistant and the weathering crusts too thin to be accurately examined. The same applies to early Egyptian glass which is generally found in such arid conditions that little corrosion will have taken place.

As more and more sophisticated techniques become available to the scientist the ultimate discovery and proving of forgeries becomes more certain. With paintings the analysis of the medium used with the pigments can bring decisive results. This was one of the ways that proved incontrovertibly that Van Meegeren had produced his fakes, when it could be shown that his vehicle had been a mixture of phenol and formaldehyde, substances not available in the time of Vermeer. In another context, physical analysis of the medium was to help to prove that the portrait of Pope Julius II in the National Gallery, London, was the original by Raphael. Tests from various parts of the picture showed that the medium was walnut oil and not linseed oil which was the commonest oil for artists in the sixteenth century. Art historians knew that Raphael was one of the few artists of his time to use walnut oil.

Another form of analysis is X-ray diffraction which is particularly suitable for identifying crystalline materials. The principle was fallen upon by Max von Laue, a German physicist, in 1912. He discovered that if a beam of X-rays was passed through a crystal on to a photographic plate a certain pattern of bright dots (diffraction pattern) would be built up. With further experiments Von Laue found that different crystals each had their own special pattern. Thus the scientist provided with a diffraction pattern is able to identify the crystal that made it. Among other problems diffraction analysis has helped to solve with antiquities has been the determining of the opacifying agent some of the early craftsmen put into their glasses. Research showed that the blue and white glasses of the Egyptians and Romans up to the fourth century A.D. had calcium carbonate added, which was later replaced by tin oxide. The technique when applied to Chinese opaque glass showed that the so-called jade glass ornaments of the T'ang period contained calcium fluoride as an opacifier some thousand years before it was used in glass in Europe.

There can be times when a suspect object comes into the laboratory from which it is undesirable to take even the smallest sample for analysis. It could be a very small piece of precious porcelain or a coin that could have considerable rarity value if proved to be authentic. The problem then would have to be solved in part by the use of one of the so-called non-destructive techniques. These include neutron activation analysis, X-ray fluorescence spectroscopy and electron-beam analysis.

Neutron activation analysis can be used on both small and large objects and is very sensitive and highly selective and will provide bulk analysis of a specimen. It has been used on early Greek silver coins and showed variations in the ores that came from the different silver mines; it probed the gold and copper content of the coins and pointed to the fact that there could have been a deliberate debasing of the silver with copper.

Whereas neutron activation can report on the bulk of an object, X-ray fluorescence spectroscopy will only provide information from the immediate surface of a specimen. The principle behind this method is that when something is bombarded with primary X-rays, the elements in the surface of the specimen will give off a beam of secondary X-rays, so called fluorescence. If the wave lengths and relative intensities of these secondary X-rays are measured the scientist can tell the elements that are present in the surface of the specimen and in what concentration. This technique was used in one case where it was desired to investigate native and imported ores in the blue glaze on Chinese blue and white porcelain. Facts available showed that Chinese native ores contained asbolite, a mineral that included both cobalt and manganese oxides; further that the Persian imported ore contained arsenic and no manganese. Using X-ray fluorescence spectroscopy it was possible to measure the constituent materials and to demonstrate that only imported ores were used in the glaze in the fourteenth century, that both imported and native ores were used in the fifteenth and sixteenth centuries, and that after this the glazes were made from just native ores.

Electron-beam analysis has something in common with X-ray

fluorescence. With this method the surface of the object has an electron-beam directed on to it instead of a beam of X-rays. The electrons cause a burst of X-rays, the wave lengths from these can then be examined to determine the constituents. Electron-beam analysis is especially suitable for the very small objects as only an area of a few microns is searched at a time.

The only snag for this array of scientific gadgetry is that it is to a degree impotent until alerted by the vigilance of the art historian or connoisseur. Forgeries have been and undoubtedly are in public collections, probably sometimes within yards of the equipment that could lay bare their deceit; but as with the Greek Bronze Horse mentioned in Chapter Three it takes the aesthetic eye to set off the train of events which ends their day of glory.

7 Dating

DURING THE PAST DECADES THE SCIENTIST HAS MADE remarkable advances to break through the mystery of age. Techniques have been worked out that can establish definite leads to time zones during which an object could have been made. Unfortunately with the possible exception of dendrochronology, tree-ring dating, they cannot yet be a great assistance with the uncovering of many fakes that are concerned with objects of comparatively recent origin. The most spectacular methods are relevant to antiquities, in which field they have achieved success.

It is of interest to note some of these dating methods as they give leads to the exploration that is proceeding and which in time will be yet another shield for the collector.

With furniture, certainly if it is pretending to be three or four hundred years old, an age test for timber can often clear up the problem quickly. Serious study of this science started during the nineteenth century. The thesis rests on the annual rings produced as the tree grows. These can be affected in thickness by dry and wet years; drought tends to form a narrow ring and heavy rainfall a wider one. The rings will also be thinner as the age of the growing tree increases. One of the earliest workers in this field was an American De Witt Clinton. He proved that some earthworks in New York State at a place called Canandaigua were of greater antiquity than were thought. This was done by counting the rings of trees that had grown up over the site.

Amongst many examples, work in Germany on larch trees in the Bavarian Alps that encircle Berchtesgaden provided data to build up an accurate dating back to A.D. 1300, which allowed for the determining of the age of nearby timber buildings. With another problem in Germany, a Bronze Age lake dwelling at Buchau was examined and ring dating was able to prove that two fortification circles must have been put up almost at the same time. More than this, that the original work at Buchau was done very close to another example by the ancient builders at Unteruhldingen on Lake Constance. All this may seem very far removed when taking a look at an Elizabethan oak stool or a medieval chest, but the theories could be applied and so another fence is put in the way of the forger.

With the great increase of interest in antiquities, so has the market for these objects expanded. Unfortunately as was seen with spurious examples from Hacilar so has the forger risen to the occasion. There is a dating method called thermoluminescence which if applied in time is spoiling his best contrived efforts with faked pottery.

The magic, that is, for the layman, works like this. There are traces of radioactive material such as uranium or thorium salts in most substances. Some minerals have the property of being able to store in their crystalline lattice the energy produced by this radioactivity. This energy can be released in the form of light when heat is applied. In many cases the thermoluminescent substances need to be heated to over 640°F to produce even a very faint glow. In fact this light emission may be so weak that the human eye will not be able to see it. But there are ultra-sensitive meters which can pick up light and measure its intensity. Research has shown that the measuring of the stored radioactive energy can show how long the mineral has been storing it. Thus the brighter the light given off when the sample is heated, the older it is.

When the principle is applied to pottery it has a particular relevance. For the minerals in the clay used by the potter and then fired in a kiln will at that instant give off the energy that had been stored in them. They will after the firing then start to build a store again. When the scientist makes his measurements of light release today he is basing his calculations back to the moment of that original firing.

Another piece of legerdemain from the laboratory is also applicable to pottery. Practically all clays that have been used have some iron oxide in their make-up. Each tiny particle of the oxide will act in the same way as a very small magnet. The technique that has been developed is known as Remanent Magnetism. The method is worked out as follows. When the potter digs out his lump of clay and pugs it there will be no noticeable remnant magnetism as all the particles of iron oxide, the tiny magnets, will be mixed so their magnetic effect will be cancelled out. But when the piece of pottery has been fired these small magnet particles will align themselves with any natural and predominant magnetic field that is in the area. In most cases this will be the earth's magnetic field which runs north and south. Thus without knowing it the ancient potter will have produced a weak permanent magnet which retains a readable direction of magnetization. The calculations are worked out partly by using the knowledge that the true magnetic bearing of any point on earth has changed with time. These changes have been calculated for different parts of the world. So when the direction of the earth's magnetic axis at the time of firing is known it is comparatively simple to arrive at the actual date of that firing. Records for the magnetic axis of the place of origin can be consulted to find out what directional changes have taken place in history. Working with this information it can be ascertained when that magnetic direction had the value which was discovered in the clay specimen. There is a restriction on the use of remanent magnetism and this is that the object being tested must have remained in situ since it was fired, which in practice means that in many cases the method can only be applied to kilns or pieces that have never been taken out after firing.

Much has been heard of Radiocarbon Dating which has been used on various artifacts from the past. This was developed by an American scientist Willard F. Libby just after the last war. It is a method primarily for use on archaeological objects that have some carbon in their make-up. The method relies on the fact that the carbon in the air and tissues of living organisms have a few atoms of what is known as heavy carbon. The amount is very small indeed, mixed in. Chemically the two carbons are similar, only differing in atomic weight; that of the ordinary carbon being 12 and the heavy carbon 14. Heavy carbon is radioactive which means that over a considerable period of time its atoms have gradually broken down by the emission of Beta rays in a process that is termed radioactive decay. In the language of the laboratory the theory is that cosmic radiation that bombards the atmosphere has built up a constant supply of heavy carbon in what is called the 'global carbon exchange reservoir'. Living organisms, animals and plants absorb and hold a constant proportion of heavy carbon, this they absorb from the food they take and the air they breathe, they are in touch with the reservoir. After death they cease to be in touch and gradually the stock of heavy carbon atoms begins to decay. Research has shown that this decay and loss of radioactivity takes place in a regular manner, following the law of radioactive decay, which is shown by the so-called half-life. With Carbon 14 the half-life is 5,600 years.

The meaning of half-life is that, for example, if in the first place there were 1,000 atoms of heavy carbon in a substance, after a lapse of 5,600 years there will be only 500—after a further 5,600 years there will then be only 250 atoms left as the rest will have decayed. So as time passes the radioactivity will slowly be lost. Libby found that by employing a meter that resembled a highly sensitive geiger counter he was able to measure the radioactivity of the heavy carbon in a sample of ancient wood and then compare the results with modern wood and a very old substance such as anthracite which for all practical purposes has lost all radioactivity. By applying the law of radioactive decay to the findings he could find out approximately when the particular tree that provided the sample had been felled.

Radio carbon dating will not latch on to an exact year, the results follow what is called the standard deviation which normally gives a datal area of about three hundred years in which period the actual year will lie. For practical purposes the method can be used on specimens of up to forty thousand years ago. Earlier than this the deviation can become so large that the results will not have much significance.

Some of the first tests with radio carbon dating were made against objects that could be proved against an historically accurate chronological background. Wood fragments from the tombs of Egyptian Pharaohs were used and the system came up with results that were within 10 per cent of the known date. The technique has been used in many instances. It gave a time figure of 3,760 years for a small piece of deer antler that had been discovered close to one of the large stones at Stonehenge. Fragments from rope sandals found in Oregon were given the age of 7,000 years.

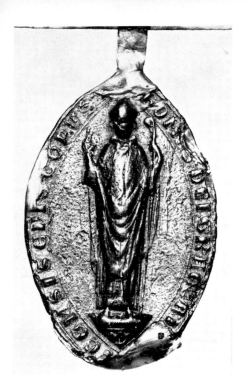
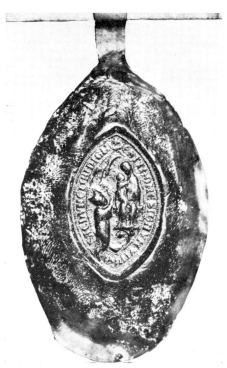

Plates 32 and 33. Seal attached to Ancient Deeds (Series AS No. 302). Grant of the Church of Cretingham (Gretingeham) 1235. Grantor, Thomas, Bishop of Norwich. Grantee, St. Peter's Priory, Ipswich. Document E42/302. Courtesy of the Public Record Office, London, and permission of the Controller of H.M. Stationery Office.

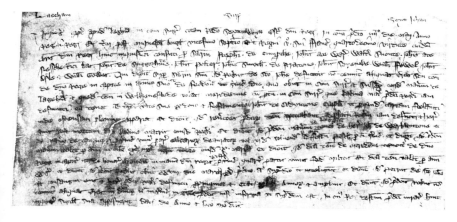

Plate 34. Chancery Inquisitions post Mortem. Edward III, 4 May 27, Edward III (1353) (File 121, No. 20). Photograph by U. V. Lyle. Courtesy of the Public Record Office, London. and permission of the Controller of H.M. Stationery Office.

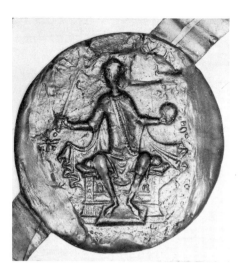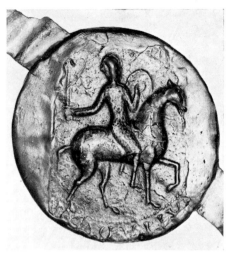

Plates 35 and 36. Seal on Ancient Deeds (Series AS No. 308). Grant of His Wood of Ludrugg belonging to His Manor of Rudel. 1154. Grantor, the King. Grantee, St. Peter's Abbey, Gloucester. Document E42/308. Courtesy of the Public Record Office, London, and permission of the Controller of H.M. Stationery Office.

Plate 37. Ancient Deeds (Series AS No. 308). Courtesy of the Public Record Office, London, and permission of the Controller of H.M. Stationery Office.

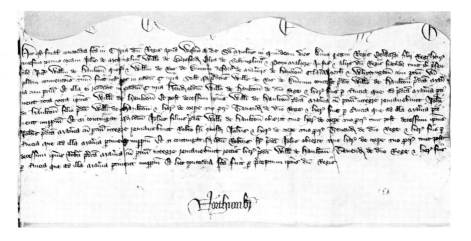

Plate 38. Part of the schedule annexed to Coram
Rege Rolls. Document KB27/463 (u/c) Rex Ro 46.
Courtesy of the Public Record Office, London, and
permission of the Controller of H.M. Stationery Office.

Plate 39. Part of the
schedule annexed to
Coram Rege Rolls,
Michaelmas Term 50 Ed.
III (1376). Document
KB27/463 (u/v) Rex Ro
46. Courtesy of the Public
Record Office, London, and
permission of the Controller of
H.M. Stationery Office.

Plate 40. One of the most remarkable French reproductions made by Jean de Sperati. The stamps (1 Franc vermilion), handstamps, postal endorsement and the address are all his own work. Courtesy of Robson Lowe Ltd.

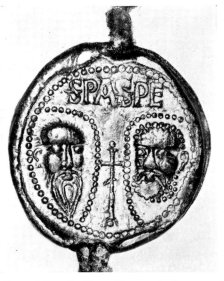 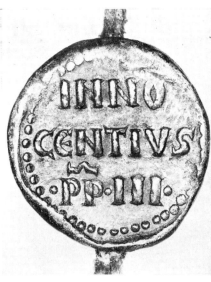

Plates 41 and 42. Bulla attached to Papal Bulls. 1 April 1215. Order to the magnates, barons and knights of England to render to King John the scutage due to him for the army which in the past year he led into Poitou. Significavit nobis . . . lateran Innocent III. Document SC7/19/15 (Bundle 19 No. 15). Courtesy of the Public Record Office, London, and permission of the Controller of H.M. Stationery Office.

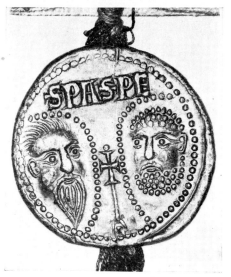
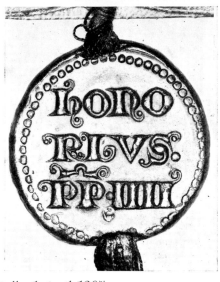

Plates 43 and 44. Bulla attached to Papal Bulls. 1 April 1287.
Grant to Edward I of ecclesiastical revenues in England, Scotland,
Ireland and Wales for six years, including the grant for three years
made by Martin IV, which is confirmed; and prorogation to the
same of the time within which he is to take the cross from
Whitsuntide next till the feast of St. John the Baptist. Attendentes
laudabile . . . St. Sabina's Rome. Document SC7/19/9 (Bundle 19,
No. 9). Courtesy of the Public Record Office, London, and permission
of the Controller of H.M. Stationery Office.

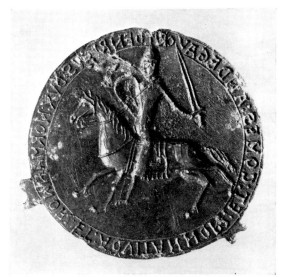

Plate 45. Lead Seal-die of King
Henry II of England, it is said to
be a contemporary forgery, the
original having been in use in
1171–4. Courtesy of the Trustees
of the British Museum.

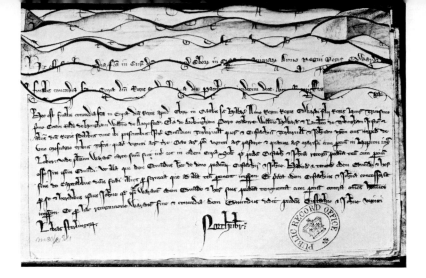

Plate 46. Feet of Fines, Hilary Term, 31 EDW I. (1303), Document CP25 (1), Bundle 181, File 9. Courtesy of the Public Record Office, London, and permission of the Controller of H.M. Stationery Office.

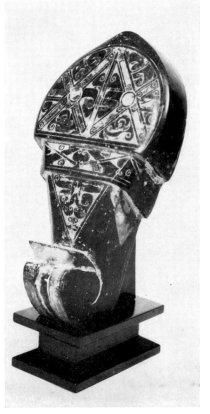

Plate 47. Belt-hook (130mm high) decorated in diagonals and volutes, in the so-called Hui Hsien style. Modern forgery. (Private Collection, London.) Courtesy of the Research Laboratory for Archaeology, Oxford, and the article in Archaeometry (S. J. Fleming and E. H. Sampson, Archaeometry, 14, Part 2, 237–44).

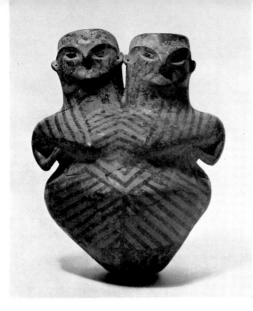

Plate 48. Shown, by thermoluminescent tests, to be a forgery; not a vase made at Hacilar in Turkey about 5000 B.C.

Plate 49. Exposure of fake Chinese art by the thermoluminescence method. Hui Hsien style figurine (80mm high) in dark grey clay, purporting to be from the late Chou period, the period of the Warring States or Chan-kuo (403–205 B.C.); actually of modern origin. (Private Collection, New York.) Courtesy of the Research Laboratory for Archaeology, Oxford, and the article in Archaeometry (S. J. Fleming and E. H. Sampson, Archaeometry, 14, Part 2, 237–44).

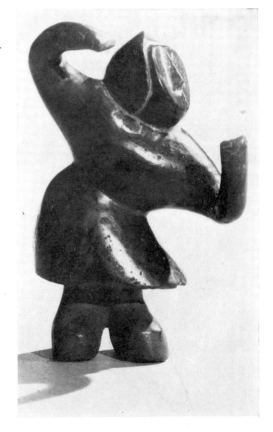

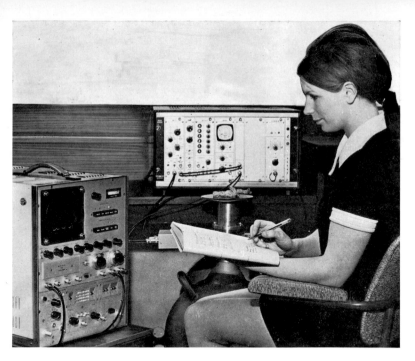

Plate 50. *An operator taking readings with an X-ray fluorescence spectrometer during an analysis of a false Greek statuette. By courtesy of the National Museum of Antiquities for Scotland and Nuclear Enterprises Limited.*

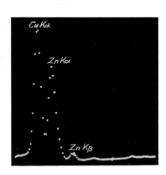

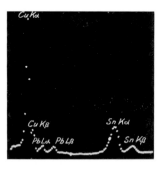

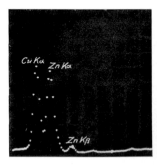

Plate 51. *Alleged Greek bronze statuette. The instrument showed only copper and zinc present and not lead and tin as in genuine ancient bronze.*

Plate 52. *Genuine ancient brass.*

Plate 53. *Modern brass.*

By courtesy of the National Museum of Antiquities for Scotland and Nuclear Enterprises Limited.

Glossary

ABRASIVES Hard substances such as carborundum and emery that can be used in powder form for polishing some stones or for producing signs of wear on metals or glass.

ACRYLIC COLOURS Pigments bound with artificially prepared resins. The colours dry quickly even when applied with heavy impasto, although they do not dry as hard as oil colours will eventually do.

AGATE A semi-precious stone of variegated chalcedony. As a burnisher it is excellent for use with metals. It can be used to alter details in fine engraving also for giving a high sheen to gold leaf work.

AGEING An artificial process applied to a material to simulate age. This may be by the use of a chemical, exposure to the weather or by physical means.

ALLA PRIMA A term implying that a picture has been painted at one sitting.

ANACHRONISM An error in fixing dates, sometimes noted with fakes. Costume worn by figures in a painting may disagree with the period suggested. Design motifs and materials used may not have been known in the time that the forger is aiming at.

ANILINE COLOURS These are derived from coal-tar and were discovered in the middle of the nineteenth century. They give a range of bright lake colours but with painting they are not truly permanent, some will fade severely. They are also used for dyes and printing inks.

ASSAY The testing of metals by touch, weight or chemical means to determine the quantity of metal in an alloy or ore, also for testing the fineness of bullion or coin.

AUTOGRAPH A signature applied to a painting or work of craftsmanship implying that it was carried out by the signatory and not a pupil or other hand.

BLEACH To lighten the tone of a textile, paper, wood or other substance by the use of chemicals such as hydrogen peroxide, or for more gentle action by exposure to the sun.

BLIND TOOLING A technique used with leather crafts where the tools are worked without gold leaf, silver or colours.

BOOKBINDERS STAMPS Copper, iron or steel dies for imprinting patterns, letters etc., on leather and sometimes linen. They are generally used with metal leaf, although they can be employed with blind tooling.

BRITANNIA METAL An alloy of tin, antimony and copper and often also zinc and bismuth. It can resemble silver or pewter depending on the manipulation of the recipe. It was introduced towards the end of the eighteenth century.

CAMEO A precious stone, such as onyx, sardonyx, etc., that has two layers of different colours, in the upper of which a design or figure is carved in relief while the lower serves as a ground.

CARTOON A full size drawing on paper for a painting, mosaic, tapestry, etc.

CIRE PERDUE A method of casting hollow bronze works. The top surface of the model has a layer of wax applied into which the details of the design are worked. An outside mould is then put on and heated so that the wax runs out through vents. The vacant space between the outside mould and the model is then filled with molten bronze.

COCK METAL An alloy of lead and copper.

COLLECTOR'S MARK A metal or wood stamp which is impressed on the margin of a print.

CONNOISSEUR One who has been trained to develop taste with works of art and fine craftsmanship. He would be expected to have a knowledge of the mediums and methods used, also to have studied art history.

CRAQUELURE Cracking in the surface varnish of a painting, or surface treatments of furniture. This may be brought on by changes in humidity, temperature or faulty technique; it may also be deliberately simulated.

DRY-POINT A print made from a copper or zinc plate on which the design has been scratched into it with a sharp steel point or diamond. The characteristic is a rather softer line than an engraving, as the burr raised by the instrument tends to hold a little of the printing ink as well as the line.

ELECTRUM An alloy of gold and silver. It has been in use since the early Egyptian times for making jewellery and for over-laying wood.

EMBROIDERY One of the oldest of the decorative arts. There are existing examples of ancient Egyptian work. It was one of the domestic occupations of the ladies of Greece. During the Renaissance both men and women produced exquisite needlework.

ENCAUSTIC A method of painting in which the colours are applied to the support in hot wax and then worked in with heated irons.

FAIENCE A general term for all kinds of glazed earthenware and porcelain, more especially a type of glazed and painted earthenware made at Faenza, Italy.

FAKE (fakement, faker. Underworld or slang terms coming perhaps from the German *fegen*, to furbish up). In art, a work that has been deliberately falsified to trick. To 'doctor up' for dishonest purposes.

FORE-EDGE PAINTING To do this the artist fanned out the pages of a book, then painted his picture. When the book was closed once more the painting would be invisible till again fanned out.

GLAZING The applying of transparent colours over previously laid pigments that may be either opaque or transparent.

GLYPTOGRAPHY The art of engraving upon gems.

GOLD LEAF Gold has been beaten out into wafer thin leaves since the time of the early Egyptians. The beating is done by placing the gold between leaves of vellum that have been dusted with chalk or talc. The thickness of the finished leaf is about 1/250,000 of an inch.

GRAPHIC ARTS In general it imples all types of drawing and printing processes. The specialized sense means just the printing methods.

GROLIER Jean Grolier (*c.* 1535) when he was working in Paris produced some of the finest book-bindings of any time. He stamped his books 'Io Grolierii et amicorum', literally translated 'belonging to Jean Grolier and his friends'. Since his time the name Grolier has been used to describe bindings carried out in his manner.

HALL-MARK The official mark of the Goldsmith's Company for the gold and silver articles assayed by them. The system was first introduced by a statute on 26 September 1300 during the reign of Edward I.

ILLUMINATION The embellishment of writing with colours and designs.

IMPASTO The applying of colours with heavy strokes from brush or painting knife.

IMPRIMATURA A layer of colour applied over the priming before the painting is started.

INTAGLIO A figure or design incised or engraved. Intaglio printing methods include etching and engraving where the lines are eaten out by the acid or cut out with the burin.

JACQUARD APPARATUS A weaving machine for producing figured patterns. It gets the name from Joseph Marie Jacquard of Lyons who died in 1834.

LITHOGRAPHY A method of printing from a flat stone or metal plate. The design is worked with a brush, pen or crayon, the medium in all cases must contain wax. The stone or plate is then dampened with water, which will not go where the wax is. An oil-bound ink is then rolled on and this will only take on the wax. The print is now pulled. The process was developed by Aloysius Senefelder who lived in Bavaria (1771–1834).

MAIOLICA A type of fine Italian pottery coated with an opaque white enamel ornamented with metallic colours. Sometimes refers to tin-glazed earthenware of an early kind from France, Germany and the Low Countries carried out in the Italian manner.

PASTICHE (also 'pasticcio'). A work of art or craft that is built up from fragments from the work of others or produced in professed imitation of the style of another artist or craftsman.

PENTIMENTO A phenomenon almost exclusively associated with oil painting. It is the ghosting through of earlier details painted and then over-painted.

PLAGIARISM The copying directly or indirectly of some other artist's or craftsman's work.

PLATE MARK The impression left on the margin of the paper by an etching or engraving plate.

POSTICHE (from the Italian *posticcio*, meaning counterfeit). Something faked, it can also mean added decoration applied to sculpture or architecture that is inappropriate or out of taste with the original work.

RELINING A term used in picture restoration. The old canvas is cut from the stretcher and fixed to a new canvas with a wax-resin, water soluble or synthetic adhesive and then re-stretched.

SGRAFFITO Primarily a technique for decorating pottery in which the design is made by scratching through an overglaze to show a coloured ground beneath. The manner has also been applied to a similar treatment with painting methods.

SILVER POINT A drawing technique using a stylus with a silver point on paper that has been coated with a slight abrasive material to grip small particles of the silver. After exposure to the atmosphere the silver tarnishes giving a pleasant warm dark brown line.

TAPESTRY A textile fabric decorated with ornamental designs or pictorial subjects these may be painted, embroidered or woven.

TECHNIQUE This may be either the medium or the method in which the artist or craftsman works.

TROMPE L'OEIL A literal translation from the French means 'a deceit for the eye'. The term applies to paintings that are carried out with exact representation, the medium normally used is tempera.

VEHICLE A term in painting for the liquid pigments are ground in or mixed with. In oil colours the vehicle is an oil such as linseed, walnut or poppy; with tempera it is egg yolk.

WOOD CUTTING A relief printing method which uses the plank or long grain of the wood. The resulting print is normally bold and strong.

WOOD ENGRAVING Again a relief printing method but this time the cutting or graving is done on the end grain, which being denser allows for very fine detail work. Woods used include: box, cherry, apple, holly and pear.

Index